Queen of Space
King of Flower Power
Dripping Rainbows

Sunny Jetsun

dripping rainbows

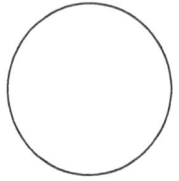

'QUEEN OF SPACE * KING OF FLOWER POWER DRIPPING RAINBOWS'

This book is arranged from 'Surreal' notes made from Inspired conversations with friends during the 2012/2013 winter season in Anjuna, Goa ~ "Thank you all" 'All In Oneness' ~ Om Shanti

Books by the same author
'driving my scooter through the asteroid field
Coming down over Venus ~ "Hallo Baba"'
'Light love Angels from Heaven. New Generation, Inspiration, Revolution, Revelation ~ All the colours of Cosmic Rainbows'
*'Green Eve * Don't lose the Light Vortex **
My brain's gone on holiday ~ free flowing feelings'
*'Surfing or Suffering ~ together * Sense Consciousness fields of a body with streams and stars of hearts'*
"When You're happy you got wings on your back ~
Reposez vos oreilles a Goa; We're only one kiss away"
'PSYCHIC PSYCHEDELIC'
'Streaming Lemon Topaz Sunbeams'
*'Invasion of Beauty * FLASH * The Love Mudras'*
'Patchouli Showers ~ Tantric Temples'
'It's Just a Story, We Are All the Sun, Sweet Surrender'
Anthology #1 ~ 'Enjoy The Revolution'
Anthology # 2 ~ 'Love & Freedom ~ Welcome'
'He Lives In A Parallel Universe'
'All Love Frequency ~ In Zero Space'
*Peace Goddess*Spirit of the Field*The Intimacy Sutras**
**Heavenly Bodies ~ Celestial Alignments*
*Feeling ~ Energy that Is LOVE in Itself**

Arrangement, Poetical license, samples, notes & quotes
Website: www.sunnyjetsun.com
Facebook: www.facebook.com/sunnyjetsun
Amazon: www.amazon.com/author/sunnyjetsun
Smashwords: www.smashwords.com/profile/view/sunnyjetsun

*"**S**o tight you can read her lips"*
The Joy of the experience being in the present moment ~
More beingness, more amorous Venus ~ in extraordinary days.
Not Old Paradigm ~ the conditioning, the doing, accumulation!
Nothing I need to know about realizing we are, I am, that is it.
Light ~ "the Sun came through at a perfect angle"
How disassociated do you want to become?
She's livin' that pure consciousness.
'Just Let It Shine'
*

Art as a Way of Life

Theories of the Unconscious Mind ~ What do You like doing?
Looking at the Sun ~ Freeing the Automatic Sub Consciousness.
Developing Freedom of your Realised Imagination in the now.
'Developing Freedom ~ of an Unpremeditated Matrix synergy.
It's more important than the Form of Expression'; Try Intuition.
Let's see what's happenin' at the 'Imperial Porcelain Factory'
Taking courses in Geopolitics; 'Everything is Made In China'.
Realism v Propaganda, setting their own Concrete Experiences.
What's the Purpose in a multi dimensional, quantum changing,
uncensored Cosmos ~ effecting our Energy ~ ethereal quality?
Creative impulses ~ stream of conscious in a Zero Point Field.
Y/our Cosmic Chemical brain! ~ 'The Revolutions of the Mind'.
'Watch out children about'.
"Watch out our fuckin' landmines!!"
*

Star Root

We are one in time ~ all feeding off each other Baby!
Nano*holism ~ Your head should know where it's going.
Synchronising your soul frequency to what is real ~ natural.
We came here in this gravity, duality to discern, your free will.
This paper Tiger density, illusion, has to be burnt!

In the Earth

Frequencies of Control from Dragons & Reptiles underground.
"This War's goin' on up there!" Dark Gravity, negative density
No more judgments, what do you want to play, still Monopoly?
No sympathy for the Devil spreading evil into hearts. Disallow!
Caught by a Federation Spaceship ~ Missiles heading for Iran!
Stopping more chain reaction! Transmuting banana bullshit;
All Our Yesterdays. Which Psychopaths want more World War?
Unifying Energetic dualities ~ 1, 2 into Zero ~ Beaming me up!
Taking them on or not ~ let's have some TRUE *FREE *WILL.
'This Intent is Your Reality'

*

'All of the Parables' ~ 'All in One'

Unconditional Love where we all come from where we all go to.
In expressing a natural given order ~ giving it a contact Point.
If you've found Your Self ~ you don't have to find anything else.
You are OMNIpresent, OMNI potential, OMNI in living it out ~
These 3 energies & Metatron ~ bringing together all Star seeds.
All kinds of different impulses allowing everyone to Shine it out.
Diamonds in them, who we are, fulfillment of Christ conscious.
Living it ALL ~ another step and it multiplies by experiencing it
Giving it from the heart becomes the Creativity of a New World
which has to be put out by us ~ by the Spirits living through us.
In being It ~ Allowing it to be ~ Cosmic frequency

*

'Underground Coffle'

"To buy & sell humans is to dehumanize us all" on this Plane.
Earth energy in a ball flying through the Solar system, galactic.
Energetic tree, energetic sea, energetic N- dimethyltiptamene.
Just Speculation ~ life on Terra Firma, not another fiscal crisis!
& something that was called bliss

<u>**S**urfin' ~ seems good</u>
Lemons are quite Awesome ~ A flippin' Alkaline solution.
Yanking the Chain...Put the Key on a chain. I'm on a chain!
When it Crashed ~ Luckily had a backup of Lemongrass.
I saw an exhibition of pretentiousness taking him in wrong way.
Police cuts, they goin' away > Back to Bandit country raving!
You're goin down! It's goin' down of it's own accord.
Don't go in the FEAR ~ resonate in LOVE, in Grace.
Resonate on this gratitude, the essence.
If you put yourself there you become it.
Off his head, bowl loads of coke! Where do you put your Conscious?
Afghanistan shouldn't have happened. No mother or father wants
to see their child horribly murdered over a piece of rare Earth!

*

<u>'Martyrs' Square'</u>
'License to Shoot' Kill, You! 'Legally' causing terrible Havoc.
Their Government full of fascist Rules and racist Regulations,
took land off native Indians to sell it back to them. Good deal!
All about War; Don't steal, abuse and murder small children!
She's gonna get an arrow in her head! Propaganda on blood
thirsty savages; Killed, good diving off horses, always defeated
by us the good guys! Praise the Lord and Pass the Ammunition

*

<u>Not Acceptable!!!!</u>
Full Shakti Power ~ Girls doing it for themselves, fluffy anytime.
Individual Ego ~ Circle of Kundalini falling in the heart crystal.
Be in oneness ~ holding it in the fire of Illusion, in the moment.
Don't they see it, are they so blind to fight for crusts of bread
outside one's Royal Palaces. To die for a King and HIS Realm!
'La Gloire pour le territoire'. They made their Supreme Sacrifice!
"One conscientious Objector in Prison is one too many"

'Regulation 2D'

A Great spirit from WW2, no more filthy slums, derelict factories empty, idle shipyards, don't go back to that, make your mind up! Conscripting women to build Spitfires, boys sent down the mine. 'An All round Body Slave' ~ Pressed into traumatic production.

*The Openness to empower
& the embodiment of Truth.
More energetic Inside out ~
No more holding up the past.
Describing it in a New way.
See the deepness ~ not as lows.
And to Love it with Awareness.
Couldn't have been better*

*

Soft Revolution

*It's not in the Press! Drop drop, drop ~ that pretty dress.
Adrenaline Concubine Lights out of the Pyramid, going UP.
"You can only have what you give yourself ~ What you want"
Gone through the immense pressure of duality to Form a Crazy
Diamond…. Allowance of Your Self to fall in that frequency ~
Your choice of a State of beingness ~ how long is a life thread?
Allowing to unfold by yourself ~ You are all in One, happening.
Female Love all around ~ the male jumps in with his friction.
Leave it to the Divine, be true to yourself. Exquisite Sweet spot*

*

Inflamed Spasms

*Drops make an Ocean ~ infinite universes on a love wave ~
Any excuse to create donuts for the Mind; Constructing them!
It's happening NOW ~ Living in the 4th ~ 5th dimension.
Felt a little Bang * her atomic frequency.
A mirror is nothingness ~ eclipsing
The Sun reflecting her full moon*

Cosmic Insanity

'They're rocking, they're living it ~ I'm loving it' Are you too?
Seeing your self ~ being in those deep reflections; Always true.
The next wave forever coming. Open your heart to fully receive.
Jamming together, my gorgeous muse showin' up. She's a Gift!
A purring sultry Love doll galloping through 8 diaphanous veils.
Power in the Collective ~ destroying the evil with Love.
Bang On! Dissolve, dissolve, dissolve, dissolves 'em.
Bring them to the good side ~ the Ultimate victory.
For this to work we have to forgive them as well.
We create it, it's all dreamt in ~ it is all dreams.
Known that we're dreaming. We used to know then fell asleep.
"We can all be Jesus" If we've the balls to step up to the plate.
It's OK I'm here, night gonna get blasted by the brilliant light!
On the Universal plane aligning with the centre of the galaxy ~
2012 Instants to change our DNA; Climaxing of Consciousness.
Needing a Big distraction from the cycle of Quantum evolution.
So they blew up the Global financial system putting the People
into Debt & bankruptcy to the Cryptocratic, Plutocratic Banks.
From Theocratic Loyola to the Oligarchical Vatican city state.
1694 Parliament founded the Bank of England to guarantee loans
to the King ~ Masterplan an Industrial Revolution, Global Empire!

*

WONDER FULL Genetic Codes

Where nonsense comes in resonate Truth to have any effect.
Apparently we all originate from the same African woman, Eve.
Value exchange # "just grow more Neem!" Simply give it water.
Fruit trees giving you their fruit for free, generously.
Built into our hard drive to take everything we can!
Bent screws ~ more drugs in jail than on the street.
And 3 times the Price!

*"You Can Call Me Self * Centred!"*
It's like putting up the circus, putting up the Big Tent.
Here comes the rig, here comes the people, the energy ~
In a non constructive, burning up phase and do you crash?
Energy exchange, have a good one and why not?
"I wanted a brain scan but they wouldn't give me one".
Normally they're telling you ~ so take it as it comes.
Why traumatize the body so much? Try the Fun pool.
A really flowing current ~ you're always movin' on.
Try the voluptuous art of Penis honoring darling.
Would you fuckin' believe it the Servers down!
"She's the chick who can put it all together ~
4 Walkie Talkies in one hand; She'll do it, I've seen it!"
"What's your name then?" "Mr. Sunshine"
*

Can be Overload
In the frequency of the light Circle ~ source to source…
Indigo Star seeds dancing with the girls from West Jupiter.
Allowing our sweet beauty to Shine with Conscious Intent.
Who's losing themselves to the dark negative Forces then?
They're All Explaining the Unexplainable, what to do?
*Realise you are it ~ All in the infinite * Oneness.*
Being the most defined beings in the World.
Shape shifters ~ All One In One.
Unity with the liquid ~ becoming.
No Control Is ~ freely Letting go
*

You are in Charge
Face your self. 'A milky flannel, mouth filled with rice; 5000 female
babies killed each day. 47% of Indian girls married by 17 years old'
"Wiping them out ~ they get so poor, they starve, get sick and die!"
Being in the miracle of Mother Earth ~ Your body, your Starlight.

Anything for a buck

America's not all it's Cracked up to be; Where is Satan?
"Try going to the other Religion and Celebrate with them!"
"How about some Visualisation of beauty? Discernment ~
fighting the shadows and living inside Grace.
Just Share what you got ~
Looking, being in the Light.
Meditating with a Crystal woman.
She gave him a large push ~ "I do".
Left the 3rd dimension for a new space.
Directness ~ All In One * togetherness.
Allowance of seeing its different Identity ~
Picking a flower from the field of duality.

*

Palenque's Quetzals

'Blame is a mug's game' ~ Battling on to do what?
Looking them in the eye, seeing it as only a threat!
Standing in front of a tribe of Primates with no shame.
Outrageous pissing, no moral standards at all!
Instinct not to have deep visual contact ~
The moment when we made Peace and left.
From living in nature she knew the Chimps' game.
Brought them a carrot cake with a stick in her hand.

*

'The Language'

How do you want it?
Conquering the Mind ~
You're making the bridge.
Full Power ~ take it fully on.
Being in the moment ~ letting go of Mind into nothingness.
Reality of new moment ~ following it * Inspired by its caresses.

Cashram Harvest

A Meditation Resort for the Super Rich with a special interest
In Karmic disease < Vedanta > 'Man minus desires is God'.
"I'M EVERYTHING AND NOTHING AT THE SAME TIME"
Who are you? Shakti the Ultimate hot chic! "I met a Shanti Baba"
You have free will, choice you believe in, Yes or No or both or ~
To the question, you experience the answer through Meditation.
Absorbing negative energy has to neutralize in your energy field
Maya in Maya in Maya ~ It can damage you, be a Master darling.
She serves him to know what trip he's on, shows her how to love.
He destroys Ignorance ~ false ego, he's married to nature in her.
Guru Channel of SIVA

*

Skulls of Rebirth

Holding tight a Demon, cutting the head off False Ego, to Death.
Easy red meat walking down the street; Where's the hard ones?
Life is full of Infinite surprises ~ Potentialities of your Hologram*
We make our own picture, he put the jet in a different dimension.
Stepped on & off the Magic carpet ~ Embracing all the movies!
Getting out of the way for an Open heart ~ Celebration allowed
to go, let it happen, relax, is it catchin' ~ in the Love Turbine

*

"When It works I enjoy it"

"You've got your orders; Now go and drop these bombs in that
Kindergarten, shoot those children, annihilate all the girls!"
Follow your chain of command "Yes Sir!" Or get a bullet too!
"I'm from a long line of martyrs" "Why not tell me the truth?"
"I'm happy, I'm only human, I fell in love with her loveliness"
"People often hurt unconsciously the ones they really love"
Why are you crying darling? "You left me with a broken heart"
Switch to Empty ~ Love Space; Please don't make me feel guilty.

Fidel Opportunities
'Come to Goa everything gets you High'
As Psychedelic as you like ~ Mr. Super Flamboyant.
Driving to the beach in a surrealistic purple helmet.
Birds of Paradise ~ beauty all around us.
A dream city for many people ~
They saw the diamond in him.
Wet and Joyful all the time

*

E*Static Energies ~ Hyper Sensitivity
The Old is no more and the New is not there.
Not in that Form ~ we can work on it holistically.
Unfolding ~ so don't get involved, seeing the whole.
Lots of different angels ~ 5th D. experience on you
through DNA holding up Higher invisible frequency.
"He's different now"~ The light is different in his eye.
Accept ourselves as we are ~ the change ~ this new now

*

Sparkling Uranus
They're weaving a web down there, talkin' the talk; No blame
no shame. Totters on the edge of death, havin' chronic thought.
When you have found it in yourself then your Soul mate
will come ~ allowing, thinking & feeling as you are.
It was once Against the law Not to grow hemp seeds!
Discern if it comes from your Heart & Love.
You don't have to do anything ~ just look at Your self, respect
be in the moment ~ go for it ~ being a divine aspect.
Cleansing NanoCrystals with the Violet flame ~ so more light,
enlightenment ~ You are your own God ~ Omnipresence.
Your diamond is polluted with the 'Identification' we give it.
Makes you feel there's nothing you can do ~
Listening to the spheres ~ OK if in the moment

Inter Galactic Gelati

Sitting in a true space loving the Divine ~ invoking pure, refine.
Direct actions dissolving the Knowing ~ flipside... Bum Bole!
"He's shooting people who want to give him money!"
Vibrations of the Crystal skulls if you're holding it in your hand.
Immunity fighting off the Invaders, reflections of Consciousness.
You see an Owl ~ you see Lakshmi; Prosperity flyin' in the dark.
It's natural and it finds its way ~ we're all in one Pot!
'I knew what I needed and I know what you wanted'
"God You have how many slaves?" Licking, sucking, fucking
each other....Raw naked intelligence ~ blissful Innocence!

*

"I wanna stroke my Psychedelic Concubine"
"You are my ecstasy, kiss ~ You are my superb bliss"
Getting knowledge of being Orgasmic 5 or 6 times.
More to the point ~ she's never gonna be satisfied!
If I'm sat in your lap and you're feeding me mashed bananas
I'd be feeling OK!

*

Being Guided By A Construct

Nation using its people as Collateral to pay off its debts!
Gotta get your head around the illusion of Contract Law.
Not related to Free Individuals. I didn't sign my Birth Certificate!
What is your Intention apart from making me pay you direct Tax?
Signed into the Matrix by default once I was born into this Life.
"I AM A FREE MAN!" "Yeah ring the other one!"
"Yu don't wanna be doin' that do yu?
Doing it for the experience, let it be.
Direct to the stars ~ the twinkley bobs

*

'The Golden Rings'
Their Ball & Chain!

Yankee's ^ 'Geronimo'

Swallowed that one, Hook line & Sinker, endemic Corruption!
Royalties' Copyright: ~ "I don't own the words if they're True"
"No Honey bees for four years then Humans wont exist either;
No pollination of the flowers, no food, no screaming wet birds!"
Found them in the 'Collateral Murder'- Scythed hospital ward.
Experts on the ground, directing these attacks... 'Bravo One'
Autocratic > "NATO. Regrets any loss of civilian life." Totally!
What sort of World are we all living in accepting this Madness?

*

"I wanted it too much!"

A great gift now ~ we got to see how it can be.
Behind closed doors…Mashed brain, let's have some fun.
For a full on experience smoke the chillum of a beautiful girl.
She's doing her salutation to the sun ~ all over me.
Low speed, nude sunlounger, stretching on her sizzling roof.
"Riding her chopper naked she knew what was happenin'…..
Getting some air through her pussy, cooling it off in the breeze"

*

Rockefeller's Chemical Suckers

"Impossible Not to go back to Babylon
Allergic to out of control egos & eggs"
Allopathic not curative only out for our Control.
It's not Information it's proper horrible Propaganda.
Making natural medicine illegal ~ cutting you open
leaving you with a box of Aspirin & Colostomy forever.
Super glued Android ~ Sticking two Elephants together!
Sunscreens giving you Cancer, as seen on TV!!
'Everything is perfect in the holistic'
Try a refreshing Coconut juice!

No Empathy, Totalitarian & Authoritarian
That's what we need is a French Revolution, les droits humain!
Fatal Injections! 'Bring back hangin!' Not good enough for 'em!
He says 'Bring back Madame Guillotine!' History of Reptilians.
Who Controls financial systems and corrupt Parliamentarians?
Letting lynch mobs go crazy on the murderous, inhuman fascists.
Give 'em a gun and a horse, teachin' em to shoot their neighbors.
Sometimes the fort is like a prison. Supreme Egos on a rampage.
"He's gonna cause a War!" ~ "Let 'em fight for land and food!"
"Where do they get all the bullets from?"
*

Inserting An Invitation
To depict the delicious joys of full power physical Love.
Nothing about last night felt wrong ~ every moment was Heaven.
Created woman with her beauty to seduce ardent desires of men.
Submissiveness to her appetizing flesh, you are gorgeous to eat.
Amorous gestures, swelling breasts, vermilion tempting lips ~
The luscious spell of her Love
*

Sociopath Contradicting A Mullah's Oath
"What a marvelous performance by the Americans"
The men and women in uniform with the big fireworks.
Designing and leading the strategy, 'no one fights alone!'
Wrote the book on counter insurgency; Brain Trust assignment.
A soldier's finest weapon in a Battle field ~ his/her Mind.
Living and breathing the military ~ Rising above it all.
Their Kevlar, overcoming barbaric enemies down range!
'To keep your head whilst all others are being decapitated'
Evaporated a village with a Daisy Cutter, how sweet is that!
Jumping out of the pit lightning quick with his spikey bag!
"He's a dangerous, dangerous man!"
"Know thy enemy, know it thy self"

State of Being

*Power ex/changing through the Co * Creator experience.*
Unfolding within all this energy which is you ~
I have exactly what I want ~ absolutely perfectly.
Got the space to realize it ~
Learn this state, recognize and stay in this consciousness.
Focusing the intent of reality ~ as you really want it to be.
No thinking just Intuition and it's all OK ~ it's happening.
Change the Concept of your being ~ Presence.
It's all just a reflection of me here now.
Nothing to be done ~ Sense of Ease

*

Releasing all the Conditionings

"This thief was guided to me, robbing me to help me to be free!"
The Sun reappearing ~ on that day, the Penguins don't go back.
"Many people's imprintings will freak out and leave their body!"
Not meeting people who can align them in Peace; Don't Panic!
F E A R is a Strong Pattern ~ melting the frozen Black Money!
"The Illuminati have surrendered; A lion with no sharp teeth".
Illusion is they deliberately lie to people. 'We Won the War!'
Now using the Zero Point energy field for the good of All.
I want the acceptance of a reality that is pure and clear.
Outer man is wasting away ~ inner man renewing every day.
'The spirit of darkness, you gotta pay him from taking life ~
and the spirit of light

*

Pranic Trumpets

The last wake up call! 'BING!'
I could be dead ~ I'm alive!
Feelings of love and Pain.
I'm alive ~ I'm alive, I Am
Alive

'HIGH FANTASY'

We shouldn't be constrained by people wanting to put us inside
A BOX, MAKING THE DIMENSIONS OF OUR MIND FOR US
300 versions of Christianity. The Gods' Religions all vying for
the same shilling <Fear> the Idea < that we are >All Separate.
Head adjusting your perceptions of Reality, deflecting orthodoxy
Got a letter from the Universe; What is your job on Earth mate?
"We know what's goin' on but can't do anything about it"
Decided I wanted a female version of me.
Indian wife ~ "doing what you're told!"
Wow! A body you wouldn't expect!

*

Not Under Control Yeti!

Mental movement ~ connecting to the whole body of Aliveliness.
Fighting what? Inviting infections, thinking about your 5 senses.
'Control Love' ~ Obsessive, extra possessive! Overpowering us!
Listening to them all without judging them. Light is from within.
"I fear my father more than I love him" Old school very fucked!
'In God we Trust but not with our Gold'. Disconnecting People;
Business & Religion; Banknotes and Bibles ~ The most printed!
Who's hiding the truth by giving you more things to confuse you?
Why do all cultures use Petrol, have the same system of Media?
Sports channels to divide and Conquer, there is no Democracy!
Tinkering with the dials but who built the Machine? Biggest lie,
'Democracy makes you believe that you are in Control' of what?
"She's got an Open heart, with my money!" Her closed wallet.
"Parents they give you life then they try to give you their life"
"As long as you can do what you want then you're Rich ~
Rich enough for me" Living with a butterfly, DNA'd Lovingly.
'You're there to be HAPPY & to make everyone else HAPPY'
We care for everyone ~ we're the ripples becoming a WAVE

'Manifesting Intent Is Reality'
The Fighting Angels of Ashtar Command!
Every candle will give light to the next one.
Getting the communication aligned ~ with the tides.
Coming to that New Luminescence ~ no more shadow.
Seeing what we want to put out ~ in a Zero point Ocean.
Let the Dark forces fall deep in the Illusion by themselves.
Vertical jungles growing under Jupiter's 2nd Sun at home.
Dream it in and Live your life ~ time to enlighten ourselves.
From out of the feeling ~ from out of the heart

*

Harvesting Sunlight
Too expensive to get a divorce - the exchange rates gone down!
We should all have a Fair Share. No such word as 'should' mate.
We're all Equal under the Sun ~ Reptiles moving thru the night.
Leisure & Pleasure in abundance; It made my day, full sunshine.
It's the end of the World ~ life goes on, it's called 'R/Evolution'
Big brother's around! We make a Temple ~ Harmonise our Vision.
Light workers carrying a candle, illuminating our dreams

*

Sharing the Love
It's your Love child, the most important ingredient!
Tantric tongues ~ lips to lips, lighting all Chiaroscuro Creation.
Standing in the fire burning all our shadows, Love vibrations
in 'La kech' ~ holding the sparkling diamond in our heart.
The Sun is melting ~ Celebrating death, letting go, moving on ~.
Get everybody on board ~ Proper direction through the Cosmos.
Tune into this Subconscious energy channel ~ Transmute human
Inspiration ~ We're going ever closer to your Inner * light beam.
As shadows disappear, a new moment ~ frequency of lucid dream.
Illusions falling away ~ electromagnetic fields becoming Crystals.

<u>"Is every drop of water the same size?"</u>
No point in feeling if you can't feel ~ no sensitivity in the aura.
"I always knew I was searching for something that wasn't there"
"What's the point of disrupting the class?" Sat there invisibly.
"What do you wanna go to India for it's full of Packies" ~
my mechanic said. "I was speechless, didn't know what to say"
"I thought they all behaved like righteous Jehovah witnesses!"
'I'm great at stews, goulash, crusty bread & butter to die for!'
Being in Love ~ Is Pain Relief
*
<u>'Mandy makes you Randy'</u>
"OK so I was wrong and it's all bollocks! Now you know!"
You're recalibrating the flip out ~ 'Patience is a Virtue'
Hypnotic sleeping pills giving you a lot of abuse.
She was in touch with Shiva ~ Forgiving…
The energy taking over ~ she was Loved Up.
On the Ecstasy, goin' fuckin' mental; Code on the M25.
"We're in the area, floating around, holding it down"
So you know the rave is on!
*
<u>Feeling Great</u>
Golden cobras & a green sky dragons blowing cosmic fire.
"As things are opening up more borders are closing down"
Chilled in Goa, having Anxiety attacks in the Post office in UK!
Neurotransmission, Brain chemistry, Natural High, balancing ~
Joy ~ What a laugh, what a good bit of Fun; A surfer's widow.
"Better to be an Acidhead than workin' fury in a foundry"
"No chillums in that field!" "If it feels good keep doing it,
if it don't feel good get the fuck outta there" Immediately!
Bounced in ~ 'bish bash bosh'. Fit the feelin' better.
'Fusion Place' ~ It's a Fun City

Cosmic * Inshallah

Uniform <> Conditions >Who is a modern Witch doctor?*
The veil is another illusion of duality ~ Separation not Unity.
Dividing & Conquering, subtle psychological programming!
Divine spirit is One don't need any special Identity from me ~
You'll legally be murdered for burning pages of their holy book!
I'm gonna lick you 'til you SCREAM!! Loving your Cunnilingus.
The Universe Made it ~ I got juiced up with a salacious hand maid.
And he said, "dad get me, buy me yonder Yemeni slave girl"
"I'm not a professional Slave trainer son" Do you want a hierodule?
'Hieros Gamos' ~ was the ultimate expression of what is termed
'Temple prostitution' where a man visited a desirous, sexy Priestess
*in order to receive **'gnosis'** to experience the divine for himself ~*
through the act of sacred sexual Love making' ~ Hardcore Angel

*

Hippydrome Mosaics

Sense of Realism at the Circus ~
"You are excelling with your fica"
Sense of Psychology in the Arena.
Cherubs with Love spears and bow.
A spectacular place for a bliss orgy.
Quite delightful ~ this is the path.
Looking at lapping waves and Moons.
Inside a seaside villa

*

"You wash it I'll suck it"

There is Magical bliss in my pussy waiting for you ~ Maybe
for a Lemon cake I would let you come over my nipples!
When, where, I'm waiting to do Puja on you. Embracing full
Shakti's power. When the Lotuses bloom the Moon fills them
with deep penetrating light. Yin becoming Yang ~ All in One

Domestic Bliss
For me It's amazing to be sitting here right now writing this.
Before there was no reason. I'd be sitting there thinking…
what the fuck are you doing? Go and do the washing up ~
Now I'm embracing a Love Blessing
*

Angelic Orgasmic
All my Inspiration has come from reaming you here.
I love being Inside with you ~ creating a Love Union.
Stroking your hair, licking your lips, kissing your sacred Temple
of infinite pleasures & delights. "I think I'd better
make a spliff, have some chocolate, then go to bed….."
You release a flood of Cupid's raindrops into my mouth.
My sperm's telepathic your erect nipples are telepathic too!
"I forgot about your delicious sweet tongue"
Gets you into a different dimension ~
And that's cumming from the heart
Choclit Creative togetherness ~
I'm having so much pleasure in my pussy I don't want you to stop
*

You're Psychedelic Not A Terrorist!
Bing bang bum, expanding energy ~ my Cock!
*'Blowing your Brains out with multi * Orgasms!'*
Cut the Top off & suck it ~ crack Open the jellies!
Cosmic Assassination ~ Spontaneous combustion.
Wet, smiley and juicy, dripping in fellation auroras.
I've 'Become' enslaved or enlightened in your pussy!
Humble ~ Open Heart. "You said I would" Inevitably.
That's my gorgeous Zen. Powers that be ~ Bowed head.
Helping me to rebuild my nervous system, trusting the Universe
for the best of all ~ Celestial Ecstasies

Paraphrased from 'Guardian' 2/7/2012; James Moore/Outlook
'Justice' was severe and swift for those who rioted in London,
summer 2011 but those who burned the British economy and
the financial markets by reckless gambling or by trying to rig
the Libor interest rates are likely to escape a similar fate.
Serious fraud squad has a mixed record in securing convictions
even in cases that can be effectively pursued against Barclays
traders. The Financial services Authority and its successor the
Financial Conduct Authority might get round to handing out
bans and fines but it's uncertain. It has lost people's respect.
Politicians are calling for a public enquiry. It needs a thorough
review of the legal framework of this type of white collar crime.
British Banking regulators are not feared they're looked upon
as 'stupid' by 'city folk' who spend their time coming up with
schemes around them knowing if they get caught the sanctions
they face will be limited and they'll get paid off. There is no
Extraordinary Rendition, the US might possibly use their lop-
sided extradition treaty to prosecute these Global predators.'
Today the cases are too numerous, from our Major banks, criminal
Pharmaceutical companies, Insurance companies, MP's Expenses
scandals, but rioters still get 6 months for stealing a loaf of bread!
Does anyone have the slightest confidence in this corrupt system?
"Abuse ~ Is the nature of the beast!"

*

You're Free ~ to go

'The Art of Persuasion' ~ What harm is there in doing this?
Giving her confidence, dispelling all her fears; Promise her.
Using various cunning artifices, overcoming her bashfulness.
She's a divine being ~ will become a devoted, sultry beauty.
'What a thrilling feeling, shampooing her virtuous buttocks'
Is he the husband of Love?

Lest We All Forget ~ What Is Right & Wrong
Ref: Assange: The UK has under much criticism stuck to the INTERNATIONAL HUMAN RIGHTS LAW of not deporting political/asylum refugees some from very dubious backgrounds back to their home countries if it was shown their lives might be endangered or they would be tortured. The case of General Augusto Pinochet alleged Criminal Against Humanity being released back to Chile on very uncertain health grounds also shows that the UK government does what it wants and ab/uses the definition of 'The Law' to justify its actions. However when a genuine human rights campaigner is threatened with the same outcome they're happy to use this same 'Law' of the Inquisitor to its maximum to suit its obviously fascist tendencies, national interests by NOT guaranteeing that this Prisoner of Political Conscience is not delivered into the hands of a hateful avenger. Is this another case of hypocrisy for us all to see!? Bravo to the Equadorean people and Government for standing up to these Global Powers and to protect the rights of the people exposing unjust and inhumane actions by secret governments and giving us the information so we may 'Know' at their great personal risk. This courage must be praised and supported by people around the world who demand to be told the truth. Aung san suu kyi said
"One Political Prisoner of Conscience is one too many"
We must show our support for the maxim; Democratic guarantee
'THE TRUTH IS WHAT SHOWS US WE'RE ALREADY FREE'
*
Whistleblower: discloses information he or she believes evidences violation of any law, rule or regulation. Gross mismanagement. Gross waste of funds. An abuse of authority. A substantial and specific danger to public health, safety. Contact www.OSG.GOV

GlaxoSmithKline; 'bribed doctors' Guardian 2/7/2012
'**GSK** *the UK's largest drug maker, tricked and bribed doctors into prescribing children with dangerous antidepressants.*
*The company will pay $3 billion to settle a slew of charges in the US after admitting a multi-year criminal scheme to hide unhelpful scientific evidence, manipulate articles in medical journals and lavish gifts on sympathetic doctors. The drug at the centre of the scheme, the blockbuster pill Paxil; Seroxat in UK has since been banned for use by children because it can make them suicidal. Company managers all the way to **GSK**'s CEO, will have their pay and bonuses clawed back if there is any further wrongdoing, under the terms of a wide-ranging settlement with Department of Justice.*
GSK. *admitted illegally marketing several of its drugs for uses that had not been approved by safety regulators and documents released detailed luxurious conferences in exotic climes where paid-for scientific speakers hyped conclusions of dubious academic papers.*
GSK *held eight Paxil forum events in California, Puerto Rico and Hawaii where hundreds of doctors were treated to sailing, diving, horse riding, deep sea fishing, balloon rides and spa treatments & given $750 in cash, an 'honorarium'. Paxil once **GSK's** best-selling drug was never approved for use by children. The settlement of $1billion in criminal fines, $2 billion in civil penalties also resolved claims that **GSK** billed government-run health care plans too much for many drugs. The infractions: The company pleaded guilty to criminal charges related to the marketing of Paxil for use by children between 1999 and 2003 when it failed to reveal the existence of two scientific studies that showed the drug was ineffective in treating childhood depression; cut out important caveats and over hyped the conclusions of a third study.*
***T**hese Corporations and Banks are bedeviled with **M**ajor Criminal activities and Only being fined! No one is Jailed ~ **W**HY IS THIS?*

Our Subjects!
It's a criminal offence to put a fuckin' yoghurt pot in the wrong bin.
What about modern terrorizing mercenary fleets, slaughtering?
'Laws that were the beginning of a dialogue
between the Rulers and the ravaged people'
'Children of 9 years in Britain were hanged up
to Charles Dickens' time for theft!' Of what!?
"Even when I'm dead I won't forget about you"
*

Exquisite Adornment Phraseology
Inviting Reality ~ Chaos at the 'Psychiatric Institute'
Frankly say what's in you, write to your beloved muse.
Angels enjoying themselves ~ in a meditation exercise.
'Poetry is not prose ~ Rhythmic articulation of feeling,
pulsating inside, sub*conscious meaning makes absolute sense.
'Now or never' ~ He put his arms around me and gave me love.
Showering her with diamonds. Accepted in my life completely;
Not Intimidated by social platforms, not confessing to conform.
Still trying to act normal what's your definition of heart's desire?
Doing whatever I want, whenever I want, with whomever I want.
*

Private – Pirate - Castles
Cash for Trash, Boom to Bust, Engineered Economic Crash.
Speculators' Greed, the Criminal Political Elite's bent rules!
Corruption: An Art of Creative Accounting and You Control us!
Banks colluding with Governments to Hide their Public deficits!
Override Capitalism added Myth; No Liquidity more borrowing.
Mr. Gandhi what do you think of Democracy? 'It's a good Idea.'
"I voted for people who told me nothing but lies!"
"He's a free spirit in his own room"

<u>Wanted: Practical Dreamers</u>

'The essence of Uselessness'~ Not for profit, no meaning there!
Kick him out the Kingdom, uniform, matrix, system, laboratory.
Dadaists taking snaps of the impossible serving it up for dinner.
Lets turn it all on its head, paradox, contradiction, conditioning.
What's the calamity, lobster's metamorphosis into a telephone?
Let imagination, language, motivations, intent, will, definitions,
names, desire, paradigms, ideals, beliefs, values, drives run free.
In the beginning was the word ~ Change the Icon, subtext, apps.
Into something NEW

*

<u>Psyche Magic to Experience.</u>

Sorcerer's delight ~ free the Mind, giving Unconditional Love
Putting the little things, the dramas into the Cosmic picture
Planting trees in beautiful harmony ~ Auras of a forest glade.
'In quietness we can all hear more' ~ Live energetic space.
Every aspect of nature singing, sense of freedom in the air.
Climbed the Wonder wall for a peak ~
Let's inspire each other with this energy.
Power of its own to transcend our gravity.
High flying through the sky with golden wings.
Meditating in joy on the truth spectrum, living Free.
He decorated the whole house with wild flowers.
"A beautiful moment of feeling for me"
Jelly Magic ~ Is always having Fun

*

<u>So Be It</u>

Knowing the way a Mind works! Multi*dimensionally Conscious.
Realising the consequences ~ Allowing Observation, Awareness.
Missed call! Anybody who says patronizingly... "I could do that"
"Well you didn't did you?" "He did, so Fuck Off!"

Hosting Titania <:> Any Moment
Civilisation there before the lost trees!
Cupid's blue bell glade under a flight path.
Hanging out with cool people is a good life.
Hanging out with a pleasure pussy is a good life.
Hanging out with your marvelous concubine is a great life
~ a more passionate wife who doesn't cook and clean.
What's the matter with being crazy, I mean lazy?
You're proud of your sexuality, your gorgeous arse!
Your supra subliminal, celestial golden paradox
*

*Originally * Heavenly*
Squirting into a hypnotic pussy ~ going up in a blaze!
Eros' Love Caravan rocking ~ in the cherry grove.
Escaping from the Parrot Hotel of Association.
She inherited a very cosy Yurt.
Garden full of purple carrots.
A hotbed of forbidden fruits.
Tantric Love off the Scale.
"I'm glad I ate her raw"
*

Seduced me on the train to L'une de Miel
"I got that position ~ Yoni Yogini, Sexy Geisha Vortices!"
"You're my Raspberry nipple slave" Multi Organically ~
She's full ~ of surprises. It was, it is, we are One here now.
Giving Adam a great blow job down by the old apple tree.
Cast out into the wilderness for bighting & swallowing it!
"I like to eat as much nice cake as possible" ~ that's True.
Going with the stream ~ flowing ~ Serendipity synchronicity.
Are you Religious? "I am now!" Free to fly ~ in the Open sea.
Rapt arousal ~"There you realized you were in Love with me"

Solar Bliss

Multi * Dimensional Expressions of Light ~ of Life.
Hitting the Pineal spot activating Divine intelligence.
Relax in the Chaos be the still point of the Cosmos.
Had a visitation from the other side ~ shifting.
Don't panic going through the Photon Belt.
Taking a ride to other Planets ~ mingling.
Tongue of intuition ~ pussy of devotion.

*

G O A L I V E In your heart

'All Wars Are One'… Be Underground ~ below the radar.
Told No Nuclear threats anymore ~ Shape shifted 'em, Amen!
They've lost all their Authority, Credibility, Galactic Reality!
They were controlling Negative vibes from the Inner Earth.
"Now they've fucked off to the other side of the Universe
thru a Star gate with NO return ticket". "I fucking hope so!"
The Indigo children will bring us to the Crystal light.
Observe, Absorb ~ Holding it in your own beingness.
Your ability to change dimensions Astral Traveller.
Non Judgmental ~ on the same energy wavelength.
Transmuting our Agendas to BEACH LIFE

*

'Spawning violent rioting from north Africa to south east Asia.
Today Fatima a 22 year old suicide bomber in a Toyota rigged
with explosives blew up a minibus full of south Africans, an
Afghan child and a worker who changed tires; In revenge for
a US. anti Islamic, inflammatory film. She is now in Paradise!
Riots on every Arab street, burning flags in protest at insults to
their prophet, a blasphemy yet when thousands are slaughtered
by their own kin in Syria there is no condemnation!' ~ Inshallah

‘*P*risoners of Conscience’
“One prisoner of Conscience is one too many!”
“The Unknown, Forgotten, Please remember them
& help them in their need for Unconditional release”
‘True spirit of Union’ Aung San Suu Kyi’s meditative dhamma.
‘Peace of our World is Indivisible ~ removing Negative forces’
‘Human Capability reinforcing the Positive, tender Kindness’
‘Who turns a blind eye to suffering?’ Capacity to live in Peace.
The Homeless and Hopeless! Honour making the Endeavour.
“Perfect Peace is not of this Planet”
*

COUNTERINTELLIGENCIA
How many ruthless bugs in your cortex?
Who is watching you to see any mistake?
They’ll take you out of the Conditioning?
Painless ~ What is Your VISION mate?
You have been Taken Over, Realisation!
Choosing which of the Identities you want.
The ONE Trusting not to be Self Eliminated.
Where did you come from Virtual Angel?
Spinning Cycle ~ inside a Galactic drum.
Untruths ~ try Fear & Loathing in Nature.
Corrupted Halls of Kaleidoscopic Mirrors.
Your Mind is Deceiving You is it not?
*

The Love Chemicals
I just try to be nice…Absolutely true.
“Alcohol ruins your drugs!”
Wants heightening your senses not Numbed!
Once you take enough you can taste the Roses.
You can smell nature’s colours ~ the Lemons.
Sharing our feelings ~ channeling buttercups

Shreddies to Blowjobs

From a super lithe ~ Labial, Miraculous Paradisiaque Potlatch.
A happy nudist organism living at the Pink Venus Caravanserai.
Hedonism yearning, Dionysus burning with a softly dripping vulva.
"I hypnotized myself with her Magic!" Your Blazing pheromones.
Are your nipples receiving me telepathically, they're sublime too!
Blossoming Female Yin *Hot*Wet Explosions in her Stratosphere.
Couldn't find Cosmic contradictions there! Vulvanic Holographic
sucking all the myths up into Kali's thrusting pelvic Spiral vortices.
Chaos of a galactic tornado ~ spinning you in a Quantum Cosmos.
Experiencing being in the moment of multi orgasmic transcendence
allowing to give completely from your smile and screams of delight
Coming ~ at the same time. JELLY IGNITED, Angelica Baby face.
LOVE DYNAMITE * DISSOVING IN A LOVE * BLAST FURNACE
Sweet, sinuous, BEDAZZLING fantasies ~ I'm up for anything!
I am going to bed to dream about sucking your Heavenly Cock.
Stop being paranoid and send me Passion Vibrations to penetrate
my fantasies ~ How are you today my passionate Aphrodite star?
Yours is the Elixir of Life ~ Perfect in a romantic Cosmic Cocktail.
I'm still awake ~ I'm a busy geisha, no plans for anything but you!
I'm free for you every moment ~ my passion is always ready ~
I am Falling in Love with your Eyes again ~ I have a Thing
for your Eyes ~ I am Drowning in them ~ deepest blue aura eyes.
From my Asylum you are better for me than Electric shock therapy,
sweeter than any cheesecake, your nipples are the best pain killers!
You are Free to do as you feel * I ADORE your natural Open spirit.
Your Intention is Pure ~ it doesn't allow any negatives to creep in.
I feel we are both being carried along by a Cosmic river and to let
it flow as a Love stream of spiritual consciousness all in the light ~
The Universe is unfolding in our heart's imagination with No mind.
"Don't worry about my Temple you are taking good care of that"
Blinded by your dazzling delight

Violet Full Moon

I wanna be the clotted cream dream for your Cherie trifle.
Living in a Love machine, flowin' in a steaming Love stream.
Psyche Guru ~ Hey up, here comes the Psychedelic police!
SPACE TALK "It's life and death on the tip of your tongue"
AROUSAL ~ The NAKED TRUTH * WILL SET US FREE.
Ask Miss Golshifteh Farahani about that, lately of Tehran.
Ask Julian Assange, Mordechai Vanunu, Dr. Daniel Elsberg.
Chelsea Manning & a Romantic poet on their subversion list!
Must be mad! Prosecution's Pattern of Treason & espionage.
Yet the Really Insane are made Presidents and rule the world.
Lust of love and lust of deities, inflaming even mythical Gods.
Pan sharing laughter from the heart, licking a fresh jam tart.
Are you inspired by twinkling stars * eruptions of hot juices
between Venus' & Mars' bliss; Ecstatic joy in this girl & boy.
Ask any Faun about the activities, delights of sexual desire.
Ask the Orgasmic Goddess of Spiritually sacred Prostitutes.
Ask that beautiful blonde in disguise mounting a big parrot.
The Art of being irresistibly true to nature

*

Rapturous Response

Really need a secretary cum Geisha...who can file, type, make
coffee serve cakes, look super sexy in a mini skirt, tutu or shorts,
organise trips to Bliss, provide stimulation/stimulus, has a good
memory for where the blotters are, is fantastic, hot & wet in bed,
in the kitchen or anywhere that allows for heights of passionate
ecstasy. Breaks are included. Any special talents would enhance
the applicants desirability. Happy to be naked very quickly and
driving license useful. Sense of humour with welcumming smile.
Celebrating our creative partnership ~ spirit & divine potential.
I am your true love, feeling you drenching me with Happy Sun
Shine * filling my heart * Cosmos with inspirational Love*light

by YOU

*I lie here with a big hard cock of desire for you ~ feeling
your lovely smooth perfect arse grinding into me with an
overwhelming intensity of deep passion. Your lips sucking me
up like a carnal super vortex; Clamped in uncontrollable wild
heat on my writhing sex organ ~ Devouring my * Cosmic juice.
Primal energies explode in my Sahasha chakra as Supernovas!
The big bang again & again pumping! Don't let me go, keep me
squeezed tight between your lips & swallow me whole, rampant
& DELICIOUS, I want to fuck you MORE & MORE and be ~
Magictisingly FUCKED & SUCKED, Cooked and Cherished*

*

*I'm thrusting my big Tantric spaceship high up inside your
dreamy, steamy, dripping, tingling, sweating Multi Universe,
bursting * infinitesimal Sunrays. I fuck hard your temptingly
inviting, deliciously purring, exquisite pussy. I am in Heaven
with your lips wrapped on top. Your orgasms are a waterfall,
molten, wet ecstasy. Your mouth & tongue devour my soul.
Your pink petalled labia unfold over me. I WANT YOU.
I WANT YOUR BLISSES*

*

"I don't see anything that's Not Cosmic"

*I got 9.16gb of memory * of photos & videos of You & me but
it's not at all the same as touching you and feeling Love for you
& Your Love for me * which is as warm Sunshine filling my heart
from one of your sweet radiant smiles or soft ~ passionate kisses.
Where is your sweetly tight arse on my radar? I want to penetrate it,
fill it with divine honey. I want to suck out your hot sticky nectar ~
saturating me with your steamy orgasmic juices is a sublime feeling.
I want to feel it lusciously fecund ~ dripping down your deliciously
soaking wet pudenda. I want those glistening sparkles in your eyes
of adoring anticipation*

May 13th 2012 ^ Tokyo
A Japanese artist cooked and served his own genitals ~
Seasoned and braised. The meal appeared to come with
mushrooms and a parsley garnish. The 22 year old wanted
to raise awareness of sexual minorities, asexual, xgender.
But it's not criminal as Cannibalism is not illegal in Japan.
In Fukushima the birds are gone too ~ there's no more chirping

*

'Celebration Not Obsession'
Each birth comes from an act of Love.
"You're born out of your own desire"
Sensations in the Portal of Awareness ~
ENTER > FREEDOM OF EXPRESSION
Dream River ~ Plug into it, the Flow.
'Clone Invasion of Planet/ary Mind'
'Can't put these feelings into a machine'
'Happy Is Happening' ~ Program Is Now.
Projections in the Light Energy ~
Love the Experience ~ Allowance.
"Fear Is Power – Control Is Power"
Over You ~ Life Itself

*

Deeply Luscious Humidity ~ "Myam Myam"
And your Conscience? My Conscience it's Clear (?)
Don't despise her! Tempting her Lover with kisses.
How her female mind works; He is her Divine being.
Understanding her heart ~ desiring to be his Beloved.
I've got my own Bacchanalian orgy, me and She!
*Spraying her clit * giant figs opening at Sunrise.*
One of the wettest, sexiest fighettas on Earth.
Chapora girls sucking a big chillum!
"that's all you need a bit of bliss…"

<u>Y</u>ou couldn't make this up Mate!! ('i' 4/8/2012. p9)
"Parents who forced their British daughter to live by the
moral standards of 'rural Pakistan' were jailed for life for
her murder. Their fear of being shamed in the eyes of their
community was greater than their love for their daughter.
Shafilea Ahmed 17 was suffocated at her home in a so called
'honour killing' after her Pakistani born parents stuffed a
plastic bag into her mouth in front of their other four children.
She was killed after refusing their attempts to force her into
an arranged marriage. The murder followed years of abuse.
It took 9 years for the case to come to justice after the Police
faced a wall of silence both within the family and community.
They were only convicted after Shafilea's sister Alesha now 22
gave evidence against her parents in court. Sentencing them
to serve at least 25 years in prison the judge said the couple's
expectation that she live in a sealed cultural environment separate
from the culture of the country in which she lived was unrealistic,
destructive and cruel" "You wanted your family to live in Pakistan
in Warrington" and 'blighting the lives' of their other children"

*

<u>Karma Nirvana: 0800 5999 247: www.karmanirvana.org.uk</u>
'Honour crimes are on the increase, The Karma Nirvana helpline
receives more than 600 calls a month from British women & girls.
Victims are taught never to bring shame on their families and it
is their duty to obey because of religion or tradition. Recent
research suggests that attitudes are still entrenched. More than
two-thirds of young Asians in Britain agree families should live
by the concept of 'honour' or 'izzat'. One fifth of those believe
physical punishment is appropriate for those who bring dishonour.
The police record 2800 honour crimes each year in the UK but
the real figure is probably much higher. Where was the outcry
from Shafilea's community? There is no honour in murder or
forcing your child to live in fear'

31

<u>Luscious' Juiciest Juicy Juice</u>

Left Cupid's caravan now walking through nature's scenes,
dreaming under her watermelon dress. I've given my lips
the intention to find a way to give you kisses. Sweet lips ~ on
my lips. Love all your Vitality; Keep it bubbling bursting blazing.
I enjoy being centred in you, in your nectar ~ the Fuel filling
my heart with sweet emotions....You are my dreamy vision on
a rainy day by the sea ~ I enjoy feeling your Magma warming
my soul ** Your hot breath on my skin tells me you are inside
my spaceship and we are ready to fly to the stars.
Your soft touch on a galactic beach is the code of love opening
my 3rd eye of enlightenment, seeing your body surrendering
to happiness, your mind in ecstasy, our spirits in orgasmic bliss.
Floating over your navel, licking aural drops from your tongue ~
diving deep into your heaven ~ sweeping crystalline grains in the
tides of your Intimate paradise, laying them on the shore of your
beating heart. Transmutation of the Sun's journey ~ thru honey
Cosmosis' * light reflected in Life ~ happening here * now.
Becoming flowing streams of conscious. Synchronicity dancing
across supra*surreal landscapes into your mouth to devour with
pleasure, to taste, experience of JOY ~ This kiss in sharing Love
*

<u>Super Satin Organism</u>

Psyche* delic ~ if you look in the mirror!
Reflecting your colour * light spectrums.
"You're my #1 Goddess Priority!"
They're doing it ~ living science, being source.
Allowing the mother ship to land in your Rose garden.
Playing polyrhythms with their djembes ~ flying sorcery
Gazing through fluxing*55 Prismatic crystal chandeliers.
Harmonies ~ feelings in y/our galaxies, sexual vortices.
EXOTIC JELLY * MAGIC TRIPS * DELICIOUS BLISS

<u>Songkran Motto</u>
What do you want to experience of this life ~ this nature?
The Low or the high, true what is your Intent, aspiration,
motivation, what are you offering? Lotus flowers in bloom.
Making a choice, a decision to live a conscious, happy life.
"I've come to pay my respects to the Abstract Buddha"
'It's not a land of prostitutes and slaves but Smiles!'
'Create auspicious visions and be fascinated
by people surrounding you. Do you see ~
Yourself as heroic or a fallen piece of shit?
"I need to get rid of this negativity"
Receive the good things in life.
Endless wealth and prosperity
Have a prosperous life. Simple.
Calmness is Happiness.
Conquer all Obstacles.
To be admired and Loved'.
Bon Voyage, Sawadee Krap

*

<u>Mind's * Secret</u>
"It's good to fall in Love"
"It's nice to go to Paradise"
"I can't stop thinking about her"
Didn't need any more Unrequited Love.
Love Play, where is the Consciousness ~
in this tsunami of bodily passion and feeling.
Staying at Hotel Venus during a Love monsoon.
"I'm not just a sexy pussy, I already come a lot"
Transcendence is Inside not all the wants outside.
The whole movie is unfolding in my Mind, make it clear & calm.
Is it Spiritual epic is it Peaceful Awareness? It's not just this Mind.
Troubadours designing Astarte's Temple doors in Novo Jerusalem

Going In The Creation

St. Germain's ascending Domain, directing Universal Theatre.
Psy*Trance Alchemist who is conjuring with Celestial Spheres.
Our Matrix has gone it's only held up in people's consciousness.
Choose after a sympathic knowing ~ Her frequency's really deep.
'Cosmic order in divine nature' 3, 5, 8, another step 13 then up!
"My method Is Surrender ~ only Surrender"
"I don't see anything that's Not God"
Intent at Shiva Valley
*

Illuminatine Ritualising

"Authorities didn't like her campaigning against Land Mines".
UK is one of the world's largest ARMS TRADERS, 'WMD Sales'
Who's selling these weapons to countries with No human rights?
Inquest, Murder, Conspiracy, Finally 'Justice' at the Royal Courts!
Jury concluded in April 2008 that Princess Diana's death in 1997
was Unlawful
*

Talking to the wall ^ WMD of a Swine flu!

"Just remember who you are!" "Who are You?"
The behaviour of cunning NWO criminal minds.
"We're drugging your blood stream ~"
Keeping you distracted from REALITY.
Projecting y/our Perception of Cosmica.
Feeling the waves of Hallucinations ~
PROGRAMS MESMERISING YOU!
Industrial Scale of Brainwashing Bro!
"Let them believe you are hypnotized"
"Just remember who you aren't"
"Thanks for paying attention"
"And Who Are You, Darling?"
"OPEN YOUR EYES SIR"

Loving It

Beauty on duty sharing a piece of your heart.
You live your lies. "You need to share, remember?" "I know"
"The only way to crossover with the 'I'~ As soon as you say 'I'
you've separated into the reflections of dualism > Sub/Ob/ject.
Let's stop ourselves from the judging, the conditioning's culture;
She don't want the bullshit either; Amazing that's all she wants!
Those were real tears ~ Those stars died a long time ago

*

Dorothee in Rajasthan

"They're all telling me to travel round India with a Baba"
"He's your Guru!" "No, I don't want a Baba ~"
"Wherever I go there's a Baba following me!!"

*

'Oh No Not Again!'

Making a cuppa tea and she's on it ~ sucking another erection!
Desire for your sex driving ~ driving him out of body paralysis.
More powerful energy takes over, can't resist; Sexual Healing.
"Lotta chicks with perfect bodies and no bad habits" Hot affair.
"It's not black magic, It's Magic!" Still in an ancient place.
Doing the mantra and leaving it to the Deity; S/he'll sort it!
Cocaine Kills the Pain; "What the fuck was that delusion!"
"I will pass through that little heroin addict village, whatever!"
Not paying attention ~ there's an Ogre, Daku by your side!
A female vampire ~ entering a woman's body taking you on
a death vibe. She'll take your mind and she'll take your life!
Waking up in the cremation grounds; Your heart will STOP!
All the ghouls hanging on a tree don't step out the circle.
"Kills all the males, no one left to take Revenge!" It's the Action;
Making karma in the name of God ~ you're doing it on his behalf!
Scared no more to Kill. "Here he's not a Warlock or a Witch,
no here You're a Baba" ~ Master of Mysticism

_D__ripping Passion_
Fucking Hot & wet, smooth as velvet honey.
You are a sparkling diamond crown beside the sea.
A beautiful feeling ~ Oceanic Wave Consciousnessly.
That it's in the moment ~ it speaks perfectly for itself.
The King serves the people, has to know how to surf.
He knows his smells; I know my Roses.
Yin & Yang are complimentary in One.
'Freedom is Love ~ Love is freedom'
Depending what you want to worship.
You can do what you like, hold it Sacred.
Giving it to a higher level to unfold
*

Capt. Terror - President Abomination!
Imaginary walls collapsing in a victory nightmare.
Made the fire sacrifices too; Whose eyes dies?
"Frightened them out of their natural ecstasy"
Demonic dark forces ruling, eating children.
A Capitalist Army marching from the Vatican.
Eternal War ~ I prefer to take some Peyote!
Flying with you in the Electric nut house.
Where's the smoldering Love Magic?
*

Bird in a String or a Cage?
Biggest centre of a caste of bandits with the Illuminati & Jesuits.
Not by itself; It's what you put in the time/space, singing wu wei.
Enjoying here & now ~ walking with Dionysus not Dinosaurus.
Pamplona ~ we're not here to run behind something we are in it.
We are the Masters ~ great synchronicity and you both know it.
She can take you, you can take her ~ a gift falling into your arms.
It's a gift falling into your kisses.
It's a gift being in Love with you

Beautiful but boring exactly what I want!
Give women the freedom to express themselves how they want.
We don't have to tell anyone anything, just sit in the crystal and
call it in for the good of all. Peaceful warrior's discreet action.
The Higher Vibration coming faster than the speed of light ~
Channeled to totally stand down in streams of consciousness.
Out there givin' the paradox away for free, how good is that!
Very ambient got that nice rhythm ~ creating a dreamy feel.
Go with the wobble with all passengers, you'll get there.
Just have to laugh, good to keep that vibe goin'

*

*Creative * Irrational * Concept*
"Get some MDMA down yu neck ~"
Yu be as right as rain for couple of hours ~ Trance Magical.
'Get your free beer tomorrow' ~ but Tomorrow never comes.
Tomorrow is uncontrollable ~ The future is in the Imagination;
*An Abstraction * non logical is an Open portal to synchronicity.*
At that moment it will always be Today ~ Here Is Serendipity!
Don't need Mind's Control only Consciousness ~ Present flows.
Being in the now the way it is while exploring Karma's labyrinth.
Freedom is there to say No to tragic ~ Yes to Magic, all in One

*

'The Conditionings': 'Calm before the Storm ~ in nature'
Their trick putting People in 'Mind Programs' of feeling guilty
then taking all their resources. Need to dis-Identify yourself
from all the sinful Identities that you believed you were.
Need a holiday and get some quiet love energy.
Your books jam up the patterns of the Mind ~ literally.
We are Robots with an 'Id', welcome to Blade Runner!
Silence the Mind so you can enter the World of Truth
otherwise you're in their 'blah blah blah'......
'Switching to a still Better World'

<u>Empowered Machismo Vibrator!</u>
'I'm tall, strong, natural, blonde, and an explosive Vikingette'
They know now what they want & they're direct*Ecstatic dance.
"Will you sit on me while you smoke that spliff!?" "I intend to"
When does culture become embodied? Six orgasms on the trot!
Let the 'wanting woman' pattern go ~ out of it, what a blessing.
Spiritual and Conscious Orgasms ~ Can you feel its resonance?
"I believe in I N T I M A C Y with Lovely Curiosity, allowance"
*Discovery of your Tantric Universe ~ **F**EELINGS OF **D**ESIRE.*
The Consciousness comes through, appears, becomes, enters ~
the moment we let go and touch the Magic
*

<u>Loving Pears</u>
In the posture of 'splitting her bamboo ~
Raising her thighs high up to heavenly skies.
Wide apart for easy entrance to the divine shrine.
Lingham in her melting Yoni ~ multiplying orgasms.
Blind with passion, lost all her senses ~ out of her mind!
Increasing excitement, juices flowing, dripping, gushing.
A man giving pleasure to the woman ~ what's pleasing her!
Consciousness of Love
*

<u>Space Face</u>
Psychedelic Astral tart which is what she is.
Subtle value exchange……Fun for thumbs.
"The blowjobs are worth the headaches!"
"There's another puddle on the furnace floor ~"
"The best way to enjoy you is to fall in love with you"
Goddess's lips sucking in a Tantra wave.
"You can't deny love ~ why would you?"
Galactic troubadours in Cosmic heat

MahaPacha

"I'm not paying to dance!"~ I am the entertainment!
He goes into rages on Valium, didn't like Tamazepan either,
better stick to the coke! "Had a ¼ oz in a pocket all the time"
Crazy scratching in cold turkey; Diazepam, you work it out!
Never seen the dark side on a psychedelic trip.
Love the playful, caricaturist, magic mushrooms.
Sacred dance bringing in the rains and harvest.
*Barefoot and happy, I love natural * sensations.*
Transformation of trance energy ~ on the rise

*

'Chongqing Park'

65 million empty flats in China! & 50 million + folk in dire Poverty!
What's Mary Croft say in freedomfiles.com about slavery today?
Now they got The FEVER > MATERIALISM < Venture Capitalism!
Which came first the chicken or the egg, the dealer or pusher,
the pimp or the john, bankster or home defaulter & dualism?
After the Government robs them they're still alive to carry on.
"Don't step outside your house during an election in Bihar,
they'll chop you to pieces in the middle of the road,
in front of the Police station!"

*

Psychedelic Music

Yu wont see me in your dreams tonight you'll see me in your bed.
Fellatio funk 24 hours a day Intercourse ~ Union with her divine.
In that euphoric state ~ ambient architects decorating the setting.
The brain's working on conflict; Water comes in spiritual realms.
Essence of your body remembering it, stare at it for long enough.
The doctors had put the FEAR in her head; 8 verses just came in.
'Giving is Receiving' ~ Intimacy creates healing; Trust is healing.
"There's a drop here if you want one"

<u>Andromedan Capsules</u>
Fear begets Fear…causes > effect
If you don't love it ~ you don't do it.
"You have to let them know your dreams"
Realisation ~ They Tell the Truth ~ frees up energy.
*Everyone being a diamond ~ **Yes**, 'Sharing Is Caring'*
Light of the Sun, children of God ~ holding that Gold frequency
"I knew I wanted to do something but I didn't know what"
Where you go ~ you throw Love in the transmutation.
"If you can give it away with love ~ Please, I respect this"
*All in One * Heaven & Earth * Paradise*
*
<u>Showers & Storms!</u>
The few hours before the Inquisition broke down our front door!
The sunset before the Conquistadores came to our lovely valley.
The night before Federico Lorca realises he is to be murdered.
The dawn before a fascist army walks into town and takes it all.
The day before our Cosmos sent Earth apocalyptic meteorites!
A new thought ~ not being influenced by the other's meaning.
"I never want to see that happen again….
that's not what I'm lookin' for!"
Lightning ~ 'Make it don't fake it'
*
<u>Venus & the Star</u>
Her walls are (damp, moist) dripping ~ wet!
You got to have the point to have the circle.
"The party starts when you get there; The party's in your Mind"
Feeling the frequency in the 5th dimension's ring of 33 planets.
Opening in the heart ~ allowing the vibrations of Love to flow.
The colours showing you how to find rainbows in the Sunbeams.
Dancing in Abstraction's light creative glade.
"We're all faeries of luminosity for each other"

'Tremblant de Terre'

Playing Indra 'Give us your money or we'll blow Japan away'
They gave them the money and still they blew them away!
That's what I call a fuckin' unbelievable Natural disaster!
An Act of God if you don't believe in conspiracy theories.

*

Candle ~ lights

"I am not thinking ~ who am I without my 'Absolute' Mind?"
Up to what you want to experience; Good if you allow
Your Self to flower ~ allows others to relax and flower too.
Not being imprisoned; That's when we start to Harvest.
Be in it and dissolve it ~
Intention becomes Reality.
"We're building the future vision"
Being a faster channel to fulfillment

*

Trigger Points

"We've known about it for years it's where we put all our rubbish"
Not just seeing it ~ Experience being in it, feel something from it!
There's something about bending down for your Guru each day.
There's something about bending down and kissing the feet
of a golden Goddess of bliss ~ just be yourself ~ every moment.
Working through us, with us. Jupiter the Giver, bringing Gifts

*

Unify Earth ~ evolver.net

Felt not in complete control of her nerves; Trust your instincts ~
"I'm Free but I'm not a fuckin Twat!" Ask my personal Hypnotist.
'Housewives' Favourite' ~ it's just another clever distraction.
*All this Entertainment * Existing in a Subliminalised Society!*
In the Allowance 21/12/2012. 11.11pm. at the Cirque de Soleil.
Earth & Sun Plane in alignment with the Centre of our Galaxy

The Need to Know

'Horizon Lunar Outpost Project' "Welcome home darling!"
'Thirty nine levels Above Top Secret ~ Highest is COSMIC'
Global Corporations not in control of their misplaced Power!
Welcome to The Military Industrial Complex on the Rampage!
"Who has the Alien contact intelligence today?" Try the NRO.
The Director of the Central Agency has all the Secret intel.
And who is he responsible to? Who has primed WMD in space?
Extraordinarily Rendered for seven years, tortures his tortures!
They sent him to the Envoy of Death. Sociopath's Conversations.
Angels in his aura brought him the Protector of the Lotus Sutra.
Different vibrations to mix us all on Earth ~ Living & Let Live!
Out of Freedom every one can be as s/he is, in everyone's own
B E A U T Y
*

Safety Net

Everything can happen, good that you allow for it to happen.
"Good to have a house but to see it can all fall apart friends"
Fighting for your right in the jungle ~ but it's all C*H*A*O*S
Take it as it is and Live in Peace ~ with the garden Python.
*

Met her in the Kali Bar

'In a hostile Universe individuals must find their own truth &
meaning unencumbered by culture' How about Civilisation?
*It did, only lasted as long as it lasted, having a full **3D** Epic.*
Gotta have the Inspiration to Smile ~ try Lilith's Oasis' Circus!
Have a nice day, have another one, another one then an other.
He embraces being the Ambassador, Blob on mate, Full Power!
You're Connected. Absolutely in the posse ~ Social Integration.
We share same truth vibe, resonating in tune with the full moon.
Joy of Joys ~ Tantric Massive!

A Busy Bee
The Mind can't see the Mind ~ only Stillness can show the Grid.
Flows in empty spaces in between the thinking ~ 'Bhavanga citta'
Forever blessed ~ Shiva Consciousness infinitely, completely bliss.
The Senses are You already ~ response in it to the apparent Ego.
'I am God' listening to the Silence ~ everyone else was working.
Finding your eternal Soul mate is naturally making it in you ~
Love is an Expansion * feeling another ~ melting in the mix.
That 'I Am' makes things happen in the Universe ~
Its Intent is so amazing ~ Sat guru playing with 'I'
Reflecting Cosmically ~ then you have no 'I'

*

Ticking Over
"Your stomach is the Boss!" Can we afford a bowl of rice?
Today they raised the minimum wage in rural China to $1/day
from 50c/day; For many years the IMF minimum was $1.25/day.
Over 50 million in communist China still live below the poverty line.
Evil big business men driven by moooooneyyyy and Poooowerrrr.
Kali's sensitive skin, her mouth ~ eating you up like a strawberry.
Destroying your Identification completely ~ destroying You.
"Why not go for Universal Isolation! *** Dance the Trance!

*

Queen of Psychedelics
Celtic Kali's disappeared, she left her suitcase in my house ~
Then the bubble burst; Man truthfully saying what he's saying.
Don't have to think in an old material Paradigm sense anymore.
Wanting to live life ~ "I don't Mind what happens, really!"
In the 'I' is temporary ~ S/he's Spiritually Infinity.
All Forms are Divine's Forms ~ nature's moods.
Shiva is the Ultimate Lord of All time ~
All the Insight Powers are in the heart * Mr/s. Super Yogi!
I love it ~ Yeah my kind of God! An Abstract Masterpiece

Astral Roots

"The True Tao is the Tao that cannot be spoken"
"The Tao that is spoken is not the True Tao"
"Don't worry what anyone else thinks"
The Eternal space ~ being in the now.
'Lots of people in the business of explaining the unexplainable'
All Mind-Object Stuff.
Had his heart broken ~ until you meet the one
you can Trust again ~ be Yourself.
*I'm sitting on 100,000 petal Lotus * one little kiss for the Honey.*
Super cool ~ waiting for a long time for that blessing.
What's happening…. "One for you is free ~
*

FORMLESS PASTE

They're going to have a futuristic War for Coconut's ~ water.
Going into Fire, back to the elements, gets rid of the body fast!
Sugar crystal telepathy ~ feeling Passion in her hot, wet Kisses.
Kali eating you up ~ good for rising blood pressure & clots ~
Ask for Juicy Rainbow Baba spaced out in the Tantric Temple.
Someone gives you Ecstasy, makes the climbing easier.
Gliding on Acid ~ it's gotta be an Angel.
Expect the Unlimited by giving your Love
*

Free ~ Spirit

You can forgive at once ~ not holding on.
He's obsessed with invisible dark energy!
Spanish fly ~ "I am the APHRODISIAC!"
'Time is the destroyer of the World'
'Unfolding all that comes is completely right'
just YOU, it's your Mind that gets in nature's way.
Just your recognition of the awareness of the crystal cake.
Expectation is always too much, too less ~ it's the frequency

Convergence ~ Energetic spaces In between
'Bliss not Ignorance!' Let her go ~ let's have a Party! Entranced!
Goddesses in an Ancient Imagination, where is the connection?
Watching, taking Care ~ awakening the networks of natural life.
The Spirit in the law. Is there a Spirit for the payment of Taxes?
Improvisation of It ~ the words just flow without Mind's Matrix.
Drumming is outlawed, banning the feelings of any ecstasy!
Spiritual fractals playing in your subconscious ~ effecting
our thoughts and breaking light into colour, realising it as
material of the Violet flame ~'Co*Creating a better dream'
Feelings of Oneness in an extraordinary 'mental' universe.
Treat it as Consciousness ~ Spirits merging into the divine.
In a psychedelic trance * Who's holding up the frequency?
Who's having the Magical mystical experience?
*

Taking over a satellite softly
16% of World's gold reserves gone into thin air without trace!
Into the background, "It depends on what Rome wants"
"The Hologram is the Missile, Projections hitting the Towers!"
They've hit a flock of birds with their Direct Energy Weapons.
Can't see a Real plane crashed into the buildings from above.
In this Game to wake up ~ Understanding each diabolical lie!
Words carry a 'Formless' deeper thing ~ the true essence.
It's your Attention * FOCUS in the Energetic Field ~ Space
then everything resonates from there as alive Presence
*

Funky Manga Maya
Neurons in shock, "The more Unconscious the more you suffer"
When you're here you're home ~ Pulsating passion conscious.
Nothing there just passing through empty space ~ no resistance.
You met your own clone's shadow ~Smile & you get a smile back

*'**E**verything is Nothing'*
You flow with the flow ~
All One Now ~ A big dance
*

Lighting Jupiter's Sun
*Everyone's in their own Sat * Guru frequency ~ Living It Out.*
Crystal net holding us together, feeding us with Love 11.11.11.
Firing the beingness, love all over the net, opening their hearts.
Embodiment taking it in, holding it harmoniously in Zero Space.
By being yourself ~ All in the Universe; Be forever All in One.
Learning to be our own Masters working with the Elementals.
Trusting Universal, projecting it out, see you are it ~ Oneness.
We're all rich living in supernatural Goa; Cosmic hazel eyes.
*

Lookin' at One's behaviour
It's their experience ~ we're here to share all our experiences.
Terrified ~ it's a long list, they've been to damnation & back!
Fascist dictator hiding out in a camouflaged opalescent Mosque.
"I just told the infidel that I Love him" He didn't believe me!
No questions stick her on the rack!
*

Nibbling that Cherry Energy!
*Om*Let Power cuts! She makes Spice hot.*
Natural Medicine (book) for other's brain ~
They can't follow you but they do!
"Cut the crap and show me the money!"
"What does too happy mean?" I want to understand that!
Love is Gold, Gold is Love ~ Alchemy transmuting violet
flames through the falling white petals of Love's crystal. Rays.
Learning to be Master in the duality ~ building your Potential.
That's where the Fulfillment comes in.
Let him go ~ that's your Love

Hanuman's Beach

Resonating in tune ~ unfolds as it does, don't mind anymore.
Everything was high Magic couldn't be better ~ Alchemy.
Looking for what's not there and killing the moment; Why?
Couldn't hold it up, turned into resistances cutting the flow.
She got paranoid going into a deeper, loving relationship.
Saw it as a rejection ~ I had to show some Independence.
Fearful of the Pain if you get caught up in her bad moods.
Holding up the frequency ~ go out of your ego & see
what's needed. I'm driving for my Soul mate.
Let it be ~ of its right, she will be there.
Staying in the embodiment of your Truth.

*

Purple flame ~ Colour of Transmutation

"Dark Illuminatis have given up" Packed their bags, left Gaia.
We all get Wealthy now, no need for betrayal, so much treasure.
The Increase of emotional corruption with Religions & Political,
Chemical Conglomerations and the Military Industrial Complex!
The electro*magneticism is different, under pressure of dualism.
"I give myself the symbol to reflect in the Unconscious"
+ - falling in the One >You are out of the Judgment, let it go ~
Allow ourselves to get the hologram of the Crystal body to shine.
Representing in us as a fractal of Mother Earth * going in Spirals.
Feeling this Unfolding ~ approaches 3rd dimensional*Pachimama.
As a beacon of light

*

Sumptuous Shiva*Shakti

Holding the Space with delicious, natural female compassion.
Channeling the Universe giving you the information you need.
Creating energy fields * Cosmic waves ~ Crystal alignments.
Inspirational Wo/man, all resonating together ~ all connected

El Cubist Corrida

Where death is a national spectacle, pulled him out by the horns,
blinded him, cut his balls off, speared the side of animal rights!
Borrowing 40,000 fascist troops from Mussolini for a Civil war.
Used German & Italian aircraft to Bomb, destroy a Spanish city.
Revelation to the World in one painting; Screaming Conscience!
Atrocity, this is what to expect, swords in the brains of innocents.
"We can nuke the chicken!"

*

*Pushing it for sexually exotic * cellularly erotic Pan*

'It's a jiggy vibration for the Cosmic nation'
Enjoying the flying ~ the more I enjoyed, the more flow.
Yeah, why not!? I like the EXPANDING ENERGY ~
I like to think everybody's nice; came here for a healing.
It's been a privilege to EXPERIENCE It ~ for me, La Terra.
You're back, have this ~ The Universe saying, "Allo, Aloha"
Immediately, tuning into nature ~ Your famous Consciousness

*

'Tim Osman Is It True?'

Wearing a T shirt with a logo in Hebrew ~ 'I Love Palestine'
'He was the most Infamous face in the world more popular
than Hitler, more famous than Jesus Christ! Don't say that!
'Another Tyrant, he died in 2002 and they'd kept him on Ice'
His heirs are still alive, they're waiting to get all the booty!

*

Green & Fuchsia Soma

The Top house with a view by the Port, in a jungley garden ~
Kama Sutra banned as feudal Porno ~ love trip gone wrong!
Sketch with a little Elfin singing by echoing Standing stones,
the blue sword of an Archangel balancing on a Golden bough.
'She likes a smoke & always has a bit of Acid; A good woman'
Psychedelic Awakening Power Tool, potent catalysts of change

'Sidewinders' (Unconventional Missiles!!)

Laos was a US Killing ground! Decided to break any Neutrality.
Fangs out, Kill anything that moves; Enemy's Life is worthless!
A Secret War, still 'Classified' with the Pentagon and Congress!
Carpet bombed them back to the stone age without any criticism
from your 'Free Press' back home, just like it's happening today.
Who Profits from Wars? The Military, Weapons manufacturers!
Who else gains from this Mad killing, death and destruction?
Then they go and build it back up again then blow it up again!
Making money. Why not invest it in feeding people ~ because
You are EVIL

*

Blue Onyx Nerve & Spacey Obelisk!

Sense of abstract light energy and shining aluminium aspiration.
Wireless girl holding hands with Major Yuri, staring at the stars.
Dreaming of escaping this punishing system and being free to fly.
Show us some Utopia not coexistence with other dismal termites.
KGB; not a Cosmonaut standing on the steps of your tenement!
Who's arguing over pots and pans in front of the Secret Police?
Full of grey people at the window making you paranoid and fearful.
Let's have a radical change! Free art & surreal poetry revolution!
The happiest moment of my life ~ time was changing. **Freedom**
coming, the seeming impossible happened, Old Order dissolved.
"Have you had enough yet?"

*

*So Trippy * Full Flyin *' 'Upekkha'*

Such an amazing natural experience at Sweetwater lake, Arambol.
I love the Psychedelica ~'Karuna' walking across Infinite Galaxies.
I don't get paranoid ~ "I have a word with myself" 'Mudita' ~
I love the travellin' it is Magic, allowing a relationship ~ OPEN
for other, other person not getting attached to anything, 'Anatta'.
It's 'Namaste' ~ subliminal Zen ~ Unconditional Love ~ 'Metta'

Collateral Damage!
*Satellites can read the writing on a cigarette! 'These will Kill **U'***
I have decided to ignore this email because you've got it wrong.
Bhakti threw me into the Ocean ~ then she fished me out again!
"Is God the Ultimate figment of the Imagination?" Yes & No ~
Don't assume anything ~ 'It can't be taken it can only be given'
*

Cunnilinguist
Male enriched with female fluid, humming her vibration.
Fingers delving into the grotto of her white Tiger.
Looking lovingly towards him ~ kissing her hair.
Mutual Love on both sides the greatest enjoyment
Freeing the desires to suffuse in the radiant light.
Let us all embrace our senses of true humanity.
Enjoying ecstatic arousal of genital stimulation.
Languid lovers resting in the perfumed garden
*

Revolutionary Forces ~ Conjunctions
Deliriums of Obsession and Madness; Thanks, not if I can help it!
More hidden Agenda, underworld Mafia Demons reading Satan.
Open floating worlds, abstract associations, sailing in a Sampan.
Liberation of Desires with Political Freedom ~ Waves of visions.
'You're extremely Psychic' ~ I'm exploring the imagery of reverie
*

Manifesting the Invisible
The devil has a big bag of tricks eating you like a virus.
Reflecting them letting them dust their own crystals.
Now or Never ~ Love frequency.
Just want to tell you heart to heart.
Be in the net and shine out ~ taking over!
Passionate love can burn your circuits ~
(Heavy) Breathing is good too

In La Kech's * Merkaba

Do you want a Pool of blood or do you not?
Do you want a Pool of Love or do you not?
Do you want a Pool of Light or do you not?
Do you want a Pool of Life or do you not?
Do you want a Pool of Energy or do you not?
Reflecting the golden Full Moon ~
Let me be a Server of the Cosmic.
We're feeding each other.

*

Threading Women.

They opened their relationship to friendship.
"What's happened to all that respect for people?"
"I don't wanna see those pics on 'mywetlover.com!"
'A gang of Samurai kitted Robocops evicting a few hippies.
Them & Us "They're the Police and losing touch with people"
Call from Nigeria ~ "Hallo we've lost your bank details!"
Our DNA Blueprint ~ in the realm of the primitive Stoner.
Living in the Modern world without that kitchen - synch!
There's no tomorrow, it never arrives ~ it's always now.
'Whatever day it is ~ It's Today'

*

Love As One

"You Are Inside me ~
You Are Inside my Heart"
Spirit Is Inside.
"We are caged by our cultural programming.
Culture is a Mass Hallucination and when you step outside the mass
hallucination you see it for what it's worth" ~ Terence Mckenna.
"My dreams can not come true unless I wake up".
I love Inspiration but I love revelation more!
Rivers of Karma ~ pristine Prana life flow

Lounge Angel
"He's the first white man who sat with a family of Gorillas"
"There are beaches in Mumbai but you can't go in the water!"
'Find your own discernment ~ you live what you are'
We separate what we don't need anymore.
The Silent Revolution ~ from inside out.
Only that way can Maya be defeated.
A Cosmic play ~ It's the Divine Order.
'The Party is in Your Mind!' ~ "Time's Up!"
'No Compassion ~ No Heart!'
'They're fulfilled in it'
*
And Jewels
*Kneeling at the Temple of Eanna * In her House of Heaven.*
"The Ocean makes your Mind disappear"
Mountains help you meditate, embrace you in their arms.
Helps reflection in the structure ~ her tongue of arousal!
Then there are flowers glowing in their eyes.
She had flowers growing in her heart.
A flow in your head ~ the flow is
Unconditional Love.
You are it already ~
Falling thru a Star Gate
of Compassion & Mercy
to the things one did
And let it all go ~ Can't lie to your self! Having the Revelation.
Your Mind is creating this whole spectacle to hook you into it.
Allowing being free ~ Not of Control, Fear, Hate & Hegemony.
"Burn everything in me that is not for the best of me & others"
"The Ocean makes your Mind disappear"
She smells as an Angel smells.
Light is Love is Life

Copulating Adults

Horror, violence, abuse is more pornographic than consensual sex.
Conditioning people to believe they are Not naturally beautiful ~
but guilty, sinful, ashamed. Negative, not their full potential to be
who they truly are but slaves to a UnHoly Inquisition over them!
Propaganda warfare, 'divide & conquer' keep them weak & poor.
So they never complain, do what they're told by those who see
themselves as Superior. It's unacceptable in this global society.
The most horrendous actions are inflicted in their name of God.
And these Monsters go Unpunished for crimes against humanity!
"It's not the perfect party and we're not the perfect people
but we're called to a perfect mission ~ to manifest LOVE"

*

'I'm all for the Beauty'

One Mind ~ No Mind ~ essential calmness to see a clear reflection.
Aloneness not aloneness ~ separation ~ togetherness > dualities<
Unity ~ be conscious of this moment & experience what it is to be
** A L O N E * B U T * N O T * L O N E L Y * ALL IN ONE **
Islands in a flowing stream ~ living free:)

*

Sun * IS * Moon

Those nailing Jesus to a Cross!
Put me in a cauldron on a burning fire!
Wealthy Indians enjoying Coke ~ "It's snowing in Mumbai"
Make them talk, give them Heroin, who wants the next hit then?
Selling their Soul for their Smack addiction; Given first for Free!
Don't you want me to get excited? Mandy it's Tuesday night!
Your sperm activity's surging higher up her vibrating chakras.
Identifying with the gorgeous form of feminine Illusion in heat.
Liberation from the suffering, being alive in synthesis of bliss.
Balancing dancing polarities ~ Aware of Presence in her Now.
"Only truly Divine energy gets you out until you're in the bliss"

Burn Burn Burning

Everything that is not the Best for me and for all the others!
They have to face themselves, accepting blame ~ as duality.
Reflections from the falling angels to show us that fallen side
and to work with that, melting the Demons with our Love.
Evil wanting to switch you on as craving Slaves…Yes YOU!
Touching frequency ~ You will see something of You in them.
You will Know ~ what it is to be ENSLAVED under the Earth.
Giving the healing is Fantastic; It's Blessed.
In the Violet, golden, white diamond flame.
*

Every book has a cover

"Dropped acid got laid in the Fort by the sea"
They took it past the limit ~ You don't need a plan in Varanasi.
Psychonaut Mosaics ~ Another Undesirable Alien at the gate!
"Creating the Crisis then offering us the solution!" Bingo!
Welcome to the Khazarian brotherhood from Mars! Where?
Machine guns on the roof of the Golden Temple; Not what
Shakti wants; The Spirit of the Hindus' ~ worlds of compassion?
Fuck I feel like I'm trippin' & it's getting even more intense!
Took some Hawaiian Wood rose & went for Nataraj's dance.
"Oh no got more fucked ~ dire with desire!"
"I'll stay clean" ~ Not holding onto anything.
Have every thing by just being Happy.
"I would like to extend my gratitude…"
*

'New Paradigm > Control Z'

Who is Lucifer and its spawn? 'It takes one to know one mate'
Full bloodied Enemies; Try some Comfort Zone ~ 'Free Yoga'
Each one's experience "If you can't do it, do what you can do"
"Who doesn't want a couple of cocktails, line of coke and listen
to Neil Diamond?" Try some enticements from Samantabhadra

Venus Rose

Petals shifting to white and platinum blue ~ Crystallising * light.
'They were gonna pull the plug on him, then he came out of it!'
Bring a bright Crystal to every situation ~ You fill up with Love.
You throw the colours of the Purple Ray, ascending Violet flames.
'Light is the source of Life' * Offering me a drop of Isis' Fragrance
*

Plasmatic Love

On the Trance Stage. 'Mayan Bliss' ~ from magical Lillie's kiss.
Giving out Homeopathic MDMA at Europe's summer festivals.
Where's Enchanted Attention? Where's Psychedelic Granddad?
"We've got disorders that haven't even been defined yet!"
They want to destroy a person's will, conquer their Spirit!
Psychological attacks made on all the Earth's people.
Taking away their Privacy is the first thing.
'Make Peace With the Conflict'
*

Peacock Feathers.

'I'm not gonna stay with someone who doesn't make me Happy'
All the Intent of putting it in ~ or another Red hot herring?
"Once you've seen one you've seen them all"
"Don't drink anyone else's tears; You will die!"
The consciousness you give to being deluded.
Ego ~ Making the Fear, destroying any Trust.
As a child of God being nourished as every bird
eats & every flower grows from Cosmic energy.
You're making a big deal out of Nothing ~
Everyone is Uniquely different; All in One.
"YOU CAN'T PATENT NATURE!!!!!!"
"Let's just do our best to fuck it all up!"
The Planet will carry on but we wont ~
I'm worshipping Surya's love beams

__Si__tar & Guitar
And he was a Magical guy
kept on Experimenting with life.
Experimenting with Free Love.
'People fear the unknown ~ Maya'
"My sweet Lord ~ it's got a mantra"
Feeding the roots of our Star Power
*

__Amorous Yonis__
She likes her young slaves to lick her pussy.
Doing the acts of the mouth ~ congresses on the hot courtesans.
Harem women giving each other delicious, succulent cunnilingus.
'Burning with the Love heat ~ contact of soft, ravishing petals.
Sweet, pure, lying in his lap with her face towards the moon.
Enjoying many women together in the Pleasure room.
At last when she is overcome with Love and desire.
*

__"You Are My King"__
"Money will be no problem as long as I'm in your arms".
"My father was running behind me with a hammer!"
Consciousness not to hang onto the Negative.
Charming, be forgiving ~ Opening up.
Heart and Soul, a beautiful touch.
The Angel's Magic is coming out.
We get fuelled from the same light.
Filled with all the little sparkles ~
directly connected to our Love frequency.
Blissfully tripping through Zero point energy.
No money for the honey bear.
'Ethics will topple Power'
Melting them in Love

Martian Law!

The fake Extra * Terrestrial Invasion of Earth!
"I'm a lustful Alien landing in redneck America"
Digital Virtuality is another hologramic reality.
"We're collapsing the wave ourselves ~
by observing everything in motion"
The Sun is melting our brains Dr. Shulgin
discovering 3000 psychedelic compounds!
The Potential of Quantum ~ visualize it becoming true,
laying the pathway to the future; The Intent is the secret.

*

Short & Sweet Distribution

O is a circle ~ taking a trip to the Ajanta caves, #16.
Completed by 70,000 stonemasons in 150 years.
"And they almost cracked the Dolphin language"
Getting them to carry underwater mines for free!
"I made the stupid assumption of thinking that they knew
what they were doing." Then I saw blood soaked Taiji Bay!
You need a lot of water to irrigate a bottle of new Beaujolais!
Distributing coca cola globally yet can't get vaccines to Africa!
What can mankind learn from Coke machines? Don't ask Monsanto!

*

Mind Games * Still

Control over Control over Control over Control over ~ Control.
Who still gives any respect to this Electro Magnetic Identity?
Trust in the Unknown, have no Fear or delusions ~
Switching off the Mind into Silence ~ the Creative Instinct.
Water of Life ~ Mother Earth's blood pumping through the rivers
flows into a dried plastic, oil coated Ocean ~ It will unfold anyway.
Relationship of Mirrors ~ Imaginative sense, You Are the Flow.
Crashing with the wave where you want to ~
"They only have to be in the aim"

Potala What?

"He's got a lot of Information, but it's not in the Information!"
You're like natural Picasso*Cubist Shamanist of Inner Space.
"I was also going for flowing" ~ forgiveness, forgiveness, bliss.
Doing 926 prostrations daily for one month! Hard Core knees!
Be Open willingly & be Multi * dimensional.
Keep your third eye focused on One point!
"Maybe she chooses to leave the body today"
Tears in your eyes ~ moments you will never forget.
Unfolding Cosmically on a lake of Neutrino lotuses

*

Swirls of Energy

With the Brazilian Twins in Heaven.
"You'll have to Powder them"
She's not a caged wild cat but an Aztec Goddess.

*

Rocking It

"Narcotics in the food ~ I became a raging alcoholic that night!"
At which point do you (decide to) break a spider's web?
"When I see it with my own eyes then I'll believe it"
Took a class in 'Guided Effective Imagery'

*

Being Both

Realising you are it ~ seeing Eternal Space.
Even the sky was blue, it seemed to be grey.
You can only heal yourself ~ Homeostasis.
Yoga taking your heart beat down to harmony.
Go in the moment ~ Go in the movement!
Conscious healing in the Violet flame ~
You ask by giving.
A funky trip!

Ukrainian Pikey

We're just Idle Worshipers then there's Plasterers on Ketamine!
Arrested for loitering, cautioned for taking a walk in Hyde Park.
"I could smell Cannabis sir?" "No it was a saffron rollup officer!"
"Govern mental is the Mafia" Welcome to the Surveillance society!
Depends on the perspective ~ Is everything always right & good?
If you want to fight you go against the flow ~ It's All experience.
Showed you what not to do; Let the moment unfold for best of all.
Lotus petals floating on a warm summer breeze

*

Energy Game

"I was glowing ~ glowing, glowing"
Giving and receiving Darshan
Joy, bliss, the doing, embodying,
holding it up ~ the present moment.
Holding the frequency of the Earth.
Allowing it ~ blowing in all the channels.

*

Lascivious on the brain!

New frequency ~ Already in the aim when you take the shot!
Powerful Ideology of an organic, sexy Apple from my garden!
Money on the hip ~ that sense of satisfaction. Dead on Time.
Who's in trouble with the girls hangin' round the firehouse?
Mutation ~ Provenance of Pure emotion.
Finding the motivation ~ of true Love

*

Lolly Pop Sacrament

Expression, connect a different style, language. Tuning in with ~
Alternative, Artistic, Underground, Psychedelic flowing energy.
'Revolutionary vandalism' Socrates' hemlock ~ Being here now.
Separating the men and women in church. ~ Ignorance as Sin!
LOVE SEX * LOVE ENERGY * LOVE JUICES

*A*bsorbng * Immersion

This old Indian string keeps breaking ~ on my Crystal necklace.
*"No I worked in **E** Section ~ mixing Asbestos and Cement!"*
She's outrageous doing her Tandava dance, throwing mudras.
Puts you in a dreamy mood ~ full of delicious extravaganza.
Cleaning Tantra space, three elves living there with Nandi,
group of Rock & Rollers & Kali with a new sewing machine!
'Driven by Greed' just want more and more ~ Punishment.
Taking the Power, not being in the moment ~ enjoying life.
Living in a Wonder after another Wonder and we have
to let it go ~ for it to appear. Not in this way or that way.
Best go up the wave and love it ~ let the flow take you over
*

Making Natural Connections

"I'm not looking for things, girls to complete myself" I AM now ~
I'm not interested going into Mind dramas, expectations, desires.
Only interest to meet your body as a body open ready to fulfill me
Don't wanna meet your Mental, wanna meet your gorgeous Yoni.
One Mind meets another Mind ~ need for conflict arises.
The Ego, Human Mind makes a veil of Illusion, memories,
*trapped in the 'Imagination' * not in Reality of Imagination.*
Letting 3D solid stuff flow ~ free sexy energy exchanges.
Those powers are meant for healing ~ us
not for making Miss Universes into slaves.
*In Thinking the Mind represses the heart * body.*
Do you want to groove if not get the fuck out!
Always fancied the gypsy with raven black hair.
*Tools to get to that point ~ of Non*doing bliss.*
Whatever you are, be totally ~ It's a Spirit prayer.
"Everything in the hands of the Divine inside"
'Quality' ~ 'Awareness' the secret ingredient.
Intention ~ Enchanted Attention. 'Wild wind flower'

It's a lie

Where we put our conscious so be it!
You gotta know your game; We already captured Pakistan!
"I've entered the TV ~ Planete d'eau of Jacques Cousteau"
'No Ladders' 'No Escaping' ~ I just walked out the door!
"You never want to be locked up in a cell!"
Kissed the phallus of a poisonous frog &
Shamanic DMT ~ Cosmic Mind travels.
"I've been down on my knees!"
*Keepin' himself happy * detached.*
"Got rid of my wants, gettin' twisted"
'Be careful what you wish for' Miss Bliss.
Overdosed ~ on happiness
*

Superman Shadow

Communists ~ the Government keeps the money not the people.
'Motivation' ~ "what the Fuck is really goin' on!"
Lost the Plot ~ Zero Tolerance for Children!
Do you understand what you are saying?
They're spraying poison over our home,
that's in America ~ they play their role!
They were friends then enemies.
Let it happen in the moment
*

Broken Dreams

'Rebuilding 360 13 strand DNA' becoming telepathic E*senses.*
Everybody loves strawberries, Ice cream, Poire Helene, cherries.
'Wanting doesn't STOP!' Help me out!
Being in the neutral gaps ~ in the thinking Mind.
Touching 'STILLNESS' in the present moment.
This is it ~ Cosmic Cycles within Cosmic Cycles

Higher Altar

A million dollar cheque on a little table under the flower of life.
Put it in a Tungsten steel strong box in the radioactive ground.
Drawing a Treasure Map and leaving the codes to be found.
"If nobody recognizes it, is it for Real?' How will you know?
I couldn't give him that, got loyalty to Myself ~ The Truth.
Manifesting true Spirit in your own way, ask Aung San Suu Kyi.
Taking all the languages and making Peace at the Royal Courts.
You are that frequence ~ over that vibration you can manifest it

*

Oriental Nijab's Ensemble

"They're from another Star" * Yeah we know!
They have their own beauty reflected as well.
They didn't lose their honor while they lost 'Hearts and Minds'
We could have respected them, they asked for it many times!
They've had a different upbringing - Whipped mum for driving!
Putting so many races together and seeing it Unfold. Explosive!
Like in any organism need the friction to make dualities happen.
Basically transforming life ~ Free for the New.
The depolarization getting the Sparks inflamed!

*

Allowancccccccccccccccccceof it ~

Let the emotion go wherever it wants to go.
"I've had enough of those deepest feelings ~
really don't need that experience anymore!"
Using me as a Metatron ~ + - 0 * All in One.
"He betrayed me but he gave me a gift!"
He realized all that but then the devil came to tempt him again.
With the flow, coming and going ~ that's what life's all about.
"Seeing things that fall away are a blessing"
Cleansing from the Inside Out

Serendipity Serenity

Why do all these failed British politicians end up exiled to USA?
Worst case scenario they Flat lined the economy then bolted!
"I am of sound mind and body and I wanted to….."
Genuinely going through the process of a nervous breakdown.
The announcement came from the King himself; Now portrayed
as a 'moderniser' in a country where women are forbidden from
having brain operations or going out without a male's consent.
This is outrageous! Shows the Power of Autocratic propaganda.
The suspension of disbelief like in any work of fiction.
Keep turning the pages, I want to know how it ends!

*

Banging the drums of War.

Who is going to Profit from that? I won't take any compensation!
Proper thorough ~ The Hypocrisy they believe in as divine right.
Who can put a price on such precious life? Thanks for admitting
that after a 12 year enquiry costing £200 million and numerous
Royal commissions; Upholding Unlawful killing by a Parachute
Regiment of thirteen innocent men shot, seven of them teenagers.
Victims were taking part in a Civil Rights march, 40 years ago!
Justice can take a long time! Does the Prime Minister today
see the irony on giving his first speech to the UN proclaiming
the Right to intercede into other countries where civilians'
lives are at risk! Hypocrisy at home right to the Top!

*

Trumpet Flowers ~ Ingénue's lips

A good question, why are there no bees?
Who's pollinating Flora, other Birds of Paradise?
'Lost 3000 manufacturing jobs in Lancashire today'
Why do we have blueberries all the way from Canada,
Poland, Argentina? Doesn't make sense to me Mr. Morrison.
Another devaluation & a new colour TV; Opiates are here to stay

*'**A** bit of a Tart really!'*
Hard and fast rules can be bent on Poppers!
Am I coming or going ~ serious and fierce?
Met a space gypsy outside at a junkie convention.
Suspicion of Intent, maybe you will do it someday.
They take something away, living neutered, taken your divine will.
They keep us too busy doing nothin' else ~ no time to find yourself.
*'I thought I was stepping over Planets * flying on shooting stars'*
Livin' in the here and now, you know.
Just a puppet in God's golden light
*

The Elves with Red hair
Surrounded by mushrooms in spiral patterns ~
Really magical there by a sacred aboriginal fire.
Need to find a crystal wand & a pixie thunderbolt.
'We are the children of the Unfinished Revolution'
Manifesting everywhere ~ I feel I'm from the underworld.
Fairy channel ~ gotta keep your telepathic receiver plugged in.
Apsaras are waiting, anticipating ~ they're playing music for me.
I love Venus ~ she gives love.
We're all happy Cupids here!
"Follow your glowing balls Baba!"
*

"The Lakota are famous for lullabies"
Doomsday Cleaners of Despot Avenue; Where's the Incentive?
They stole all the Gold, Yeah, they usually do do that!
'Sent his Lear Jet to Brazil to bring some prostitutes'
Burying my frozen, broken heart at Wounded Knee.
Sailing Non disillusioned ~ on a Cosmic Ocean Ship.
Supping her glistening Ruby chalice, she has the gift.
Came in my brain ~ gave her an Epiphany pill to chill

All God's Children
The Royal blood of Reptiles and Dragons. & He's a Nazi…
"All the successful businessmen in Russia are in Prison!"
Even the Shape shifters have the right to turn around ~
Can never escape Totalitarian ~ In the game of duality.
Living your life ~ energy on which frequency level?
"People without money are Slaves, Mentally?"
Tulip bulbs glowing in a Light Field

*

Venus' Energy
Her wet Temple of steaming erotica ~
"Could've started a fire with my pussy!"
A little spark, a gorgeous bright flame.
Spiritual Spiral ~ super meridian chi!
It's how you do it!
Freeing them ~ from a web.
Discernment of the duality
that we are ONE

*

No Comparisons
"What doesn't kill you makes you stronger" 'Repent, Vatican!'
They're really brutal, not carrying those big sticks for nothing.
"Have you ever had a soul mate stick a knife in your back ~
or through your heart?" Connections to the next dimension.
Participatory ~ reflecting the wholeness of this holist expression.
Four more cardinals going to Prison ~ Extraordinary rendition!
Blue white crystallized light, no doubt, no more black shadows.
"Judging yourself when you only want to hold up your Illusion"
All doing our own thing don't matter what you or another thinks.
Removing the Fear patterns, as real as coffee, toast and eggs!
You face what you gotta face.

'Happy Dhamma'
BUT THIS IS the Cosmic Ocean….
But there are no buts unless you want there to be!
"I didn't know what to think of him!"
Emptiness to purify your Mind ~ walking meditation.
"Old cows always like to eat young, fresh grass"
Psychedelica in the air ~ in the atmosphere of the timessss
*

Dead Simple
More female ego I'd rather be single than let her into my life!
"I told her to get a JOB or it's over" How it ended. She's gone.
Is life then just the destiny ~ of the Mafiosi? Ask your Karma.
'We play by our own rules, only break the other's!'
"To buy humans is dehumanizing" Trafficking in Violations.
Who's triggering your Inspiration; Who's tweaking your bliss?
Mr. Tarantula's War; Ask at the 'Husbands Day Care Centre'
*Cosmic Surrealist * Zen Codes turning on Magic roundabouts.*
'Small circles of Heaven'
*

Bindass Hedonist
"You can use my heart drive, play with my memory stick"
"It's your eyes they got me going and your voice"
"Love is feeling ~ I'm a Good person, No fear"
Completely speechless ~ blissed out Sorceress.
"The way to Enlightenment is through my pussy"
"I knew you'd say that and it's True again"
My eyes are rolling ~ real absorption.
Passion straight out the saucepan
Loves to put it in her sexy mouth.
While you're doing it Enjoy it
Don't think about it!
Surrender to Love.

Intuitive * Yoga

You are the love ~ then you reflect it
making Space for the new to come in.
We love the moment when we are together.
Have to let everyone completely free ~
Not dependant on the Passion but loving
your lips of unconditional love in yourself.
A melting process transmuting in the One.
Always the Allowance sharing the beauty ~
If you fall into the heart you love them at once.
We are all there ~ right time to enter the doorway.
You've fallen in the pot! Eat it up!
You fall in it because you can't control it!
You have the control when you let go ~
*

'Intra Your Eyes Only'

Allowance ~ not Co dependency > Interdependence.
It has to go through you and you own it ~ Cosmology.
*Only the breaking of the light * worshipping Universal.*
*You give it to your multi * self ~ the Best of the Best.*
I'm in the Love Letting it go ~ ALL IN ONENESS.
'Individualised beingness' ~ Owning it, You are it!
Processing Unconditional Love, giving us the frequency.
In the All in One ~ then you are free.
Fall in the vibration not in the words.
It's what's in between ~ the Forms.
Building up the True communication ~ Open transmission.
Let it happen ~ time for 'Classified', 'Top Secrets' is over!
*Action is ~ no action because it's already * In a bigger action,*
floating with the highest of Immortal Gods & Goddesses Blissed.
You go out of the way with the wind ~ not against you; Blessed.
With water not against water ~ Swimming in light Consciousness

Ram Ray & Agent Orange
100 million devoted followers and he's going with the flow ~
Could be he's meditating on a Higher frequency of Detachment!
Laughing his head off with H. Kissinger. ~ A Major War Criminal!
What's the joke? He can make you flip out, singing you a mantra.
"You've shown me everything" Is he your Baba or the Illuminati?

*

Chillums in a hammock
Dreaming the dream, right side of brain not lazy just Shanti.
She's giving me 'Fuck me' looks & you're being like Krishna.
I was a sinner. Throwing out the most lost souls in the World.
It's Cosmic nature that created you. It's mystical & very Real!
Babas living in a glacier, naked yogis sitting on a stalagmite!
Defending dragonflies with psychic powers; Esoteric Insight.

*

"Why waste your life with all this bitterness brother?"
Attached Existence of Exaggeration not worth the Aggravation
& he'll never see it my way! Broke the lock I never knew I had.
Inspired by Surrealists, painting dreams, Imagination traveling,
transcending >'That's Mine!' "Because we Care" ~'Inshallah'
In a land of pagan Poppets sticking pins in straw voodoo dolls.
Just dance and glorify the Divine, celebration, blisses everyday.
Choose as many lives as you want or make it out in one shot!
Your choice up to you ~ Coming back Master of Open Secrets.
Being Spontaneous ~ It's what you get and what you don't get.
With this one I'm completely Free ~ not chained to each other.
Just plugged me in ~ eloped on Venus' mother ship of fantasy.
Unity is strength ~ many Conscious hands making Light work.
Sharing bodily fluids, "have you tried a pink crystalline Yoni?"
Letting it go ~ Surrendering even if it comes out wrong, a loss,
that's what it is, so be it. A REAL mistake but Nobody's fault ~
She licked it too much so I was kicked out of Pussy World.

Flip it on its head
'I give free blow jobs!'
'I was a very Desperate Concubine'
Juicy radiance dripping down her elbows.
"Cum over my nipples if you gonna cum anywhere"
"You can bring a man out of paralysis caressing your breasts!"
"It is what it is, it was what it was, it is what it was ~ As it is"
Before I came across you literally ~ free exchange of feelings.
Cupid's Blazing Hot Love arrow...'Love leads him to her bedside'
'He is known for his images of powerful mysterious women'
Giving each other what you can ~ It's fulfillment....
Your Love is an ecstatic poem on your wet lips.
"You're a divine fuck ~ You're fucking divine"
"It's all about living your light ~ shining bright"
Notion Potion ~ Ocean of sublime devotion.
Are You Feeling it, touching it ~ changing?
Enjoying a bit of Lingham Yoga!

*

Closed Eyes ~ Slipping Away
Kali's Cup showing emptiness ~ break the cup, emptiness still there.
Who's bouncing on the Bananas ~ off the Doughnuts at Baga beach!
"You can't afford to live in that dream anymore, bring it to me ~
I'll give it light" "He's not loaning anything to that bunch of hippies!"
Planting sweet or bitter seeds in your garden of subconscious Mind.
Growing them with loving energetic radiation gives you which fruit?
Reaping the harvest from a Vengeance pulpit or a Happy House?
Still all biochemicals at the end of the day, your body oozing Acid.
Release your Love, surrender to the violet flame ~ Enjoying Bliss.
I'm teaching you discipline you're teaching me to lose control ~
before it's too late! "I'm feeling the connection not just the lust"
Time to feel Space ~ "Are you falling in love with me again?"
My Mind is Open ~ My Heart is blooming ~ Cosmic Shanti

Fondling Your Imagination
"Doesn't mean I don't like it in my mouth" You said that.
"Go and find the oil"~ Your nipples, my Fun thumbs!
"I'm too sexy for my hair"~ the breeze is on my pussy.
Fantasy ~ sharing our energies on that Level of Ecstasy.
Airy fairy ~ like telling the water 'I love you'. If you can't
talk to your tomato plants how can you talk to your own wife?
Experimenting in the power of Positive thinking ~ the Intention.
I need to get rid of the negativity. All Mind's illusion of duality.
If you're out of your head ~ 'Consciously' you're in the moment.
Awareness of no thoughts, a clear Mind to reflect ~ harmony,
the Oneness here now
*
Does he have a License to Whirl?
I lived in a cave with a Sufi. That old swirling hot chestnut ~
"It's not our Policy" Terms and Conditions apply; Naturally!
Seeing the control trying to let go ~ of what? Whose Throne?
"You'll be hunting me down for a blow job." Of course I will!
"I'm sure you'll get a chance to feel my hot pussy sometime
later today." No time ~ no space to spare, fuck me right now!
'Which came first the chicken or the egg?' "You seduced me!"
Time is only a man made Measurement concept 24/7 etc et al;
Existing Omnipresently not in some numeral duality, mentality.
Which came first Cocaine supply or innumerable USA users?
The Mafia or the Police, Laws and Orders or Universal chaos?
Causes and effects are all conceived in our Mind where there
abides the Himalayas, deep Oceans, Wars, cultural constructs.
All these conditions fed us to Judge and make ~ Separateness.
Adam, Eve ejected from the Garden of Eden by a wrathful God
for enjoying Mother nature's fruit with innocence in their spirit.
Make your own Mind up, Imagination, forgiveness from the heart.
It's all the Abstract creation of our subconscious ~ Cosmically

*"**Y**ou're made for each other"*
Producer.. 'YOU ARE THE MUSE PAR EXCELLENCE'
giving me all your creative energy ~ The juice of all juices.
*Body to body * skin to skin ~ moment to moment * Love to love.*
*C u 2 in our astral projection * my sweetest psychedelic concubine.*
*Emotion * Multi (orgasmic)* Magical *Alchemy, Organically!*
Enchantment Energy Making Me Ascend ~ as in a real dream.
EROTICA'S MAGNETIC MATING ALLURE.
You got the feeling ~ special effects are in your fingers.
I love it...Again...Looking forward to doing lots more with you,
my beautiful, supersensitive Geisha, YOU GOT THE TOUCH ~
*that I love, you got the look * in your eyes, that I F...... Adore!*
*

Orgiastic Centaurs
Our Intimacy ~ Primal sensations ~ Pagan nudity.
Rolling out a Jesuit Inquisition to keep them pure!
Dissolving her in the night...the question is......?
*"How will we stay FREE?" Multi * dimensions inside.*
'Projecting my hot desires, crawling into her Psyche'
Adorning her magical pool, sexual effervescence, magnificence,
sumptuously decorated ~ eye ravished, gorgeously fantastic.
A good job for a God or any divine being ~ Seizing us!
Materializing luminescent exotic songbirds in a vacuum
Lavish silver testicles discovered in an Orchid garden.
Satyrs playing Pan pipes inside a frenzied Nymphaeum.
The delights of imitating nature ~ on a summer's eve
***

Naked or with my socks still on? Keeping Love not enslaved.
I like the variety ~ naked with socks and naked without socks.
I'll try and keep sane in this seemingly crazy world, until then
letting our Love feelings keep this tantric nectar flowing free ~
and these happy sparks of bliss burning brightly in our hearts

71

Who Am I

"You are one of the most beautiful woman I've ever seen"
You are my Geisha, Tantric, Private secretary cumming.
My naked muse of Passion, my ninja warrior of desire
& Peace. My Jedi priestess of Cosmic Communication.
You are my ambrosial Concubine with the beautiful lips
and a heart of Love ~ delightfully overflowing just for me.
You are my true friend ~ an undiscovered Jewel ~ Found.
Real, sublime, demure, romantic, sultry, magnetic lodestone.
My co*creative Paramour, mistress of uncontrolled emotions,
with tight, writhing buttocks locking us in conjugal rhythms!
You are my treasure trove, joined for ultra sensual pleasure
flowing through my throbbing veins as eternal Divine Magic.
You are my erotic dreaming, sharing days and nights together
in Heavenly Bliss, caressing a Poetess, sexual nectar Goddess.
You are my Carnal Super Juicy ~ natural passion fruity.
Your fragrant, velvet Vulva's sweet wetness is a paradise
to my wildly besotted tongue, tasting deeply, pure euphoria.
You are my Amazing FREEDOM to Explore ~ discovering
more within my Satguru * in your gleaming eyes of laughter.
You are Queen of Intuition with your pussy of enlightenment.
You are my lascivious companion licking my delicious cum,
sucking, devouring my lingham with your mouth's desires.
You are my Astral partner traveling across time and space ~
You are my aphrodisiacal mate seducing me with your kisses.
You are my tender friend giving me courage and Inspiration
to confront serenely all my fears inside with a reassuring smile.
You are my Psychedelic, exotic, Star sister climaxing my soul,
connecting my magical wand in your sacred cunnilingus palace.
You are my trustful playmate taking me inside Nirvana's grace,
sharing your heavenly multi orgasms, dripping us in ecstasies.
You are my clear crystal reflection shining bright,
bringing me into the light

Idle Worship

All together now, "Long to Reign over us…
God save our Queen"~ Slaves' chorus line!
Do they realize what they are singing?
That they're the worker bees in this hive!
Unbelievable, is this Real or brainwashing?
'Achtung!" "Arbeits Machts Frei'; Was ist los?
"How can a friend be indebted to you?"
"The Truth Will Set US Free"
Om in your Open heart.
'I AM Cosmic Infinity'

*

Crown Gesture

'One Jewel on the right wavelength ~
Nile Green eyes ~ You are the Ocean
Molecules dancing by the Milky Way.
'Everyone is their own Satguru ~
'It's only what you give yourself'
In the Intuition directing the Mind.
Waking up with Sunlight on her lips.
She's dreaming with my full Moon
between her smooth, perfect hips.
This is the ejaculating Universe!

*

Droning On Corpses!

What is the reasoning behind your Genocide, any crazy rationale
for your infanticide, which law is allowing you a holy killing war?
What's the accepted will for you to torture and murder innocents
Exploding your fellow bus passengers into scattered fragments ~
Which sacred writ ordained you to blow yourself into martyr's shit
& bequeath children in the Kindergarten to become traumatized,
bloody, limbless orphans?

Where Are You?

On a four poster bed covered in cum rolling spliffs, Pizza on way.
Living a dream here for the pleasure of others; Thank you Guru.
"I felt fuck it, this is my body this is who I am, My Temple"
Psychedelic fuck queen, lost in lust with you. A Rose for lovers ~
'It's not how many times I come it's how many times I don't come'
"It's when am I Not coming!?" "You make me Insatiable!"
Her burning desire set the Alarm on fire!
"I literally melted" ~ "I know what feels right"
*

What's the point of imitating creativity?

"I didn't want my daddy to see what was in my mind"
Distracted with the wife ~ You felt so much to me.
My heart was broken as much as I love her.
Naked in the lake vision; Naked, empty Mind shivering.
Don't worry about that, a fear trap, eating up my heart drive!
Sense of spontaneity ~ the instantaneous effecting * Alchemy.
Prophecy touching the common key ~ being in tune with timely.
FREE ~ TO LET GO * of everything sooner or later * forever.
Yu gonna have to sort somethin' out this has gone beyond a joke!
*

Becoming Brutally deSenitised

'Use & Abuse' ….'Beauty & The fucking Beast!'
Enjoying the sharing of Love between two people….
Caring, giving to each other, Mind, body and spiritually.
Not Violently, abusively, threateningly, menacingly, in hatred.
'She's the 'enemy' so can be violated by these evil Satanists!'
She's now on the Critical list and has lost all her vital organs;
Dumped them beside her naked body on the roadside ~
This madness leads to terrible enslavement of us all.
Rape is being used as a 'Weapon of Massive Destruction'
Say after me, "The Greatest Pleasure Is Giving Pleasure"

Have a great trip

The silver lining in these freezing stormy grey clouds here is
knowing you will again soon be heating up my heart with your
lascivious desire, sublime passions full of sweet nectar spread all
over our bodies, voraciously eating my hard cock for breakfast.
Cumming all over me in the Passion Pagoda. Can't wait; When?
Goddess looking forward to our next dreamy, exotic fairy tale,
looking forward to the next wet, sweetly erotic, passionate love.
Amour you are now beyond any words ~ You are the real loving
experience put in life. Your feeling is more than any gentle romantic
verse of Gibran or love sonnet of Rumi. Your heart is beating & you
are beaming inside a glowing happy smile ~ dripping rainbows.

*

'I WON'

The future with a twist of Spiritual ** YOU ARE A TRUE STAR **
"You're one scorching hot pussy" ~ "& YOU are a Fucking GENIUS!"
Dripping Spiritual Love Passion all over my elongated tongue.
"The perfect is now ~ Put your arms around me;
Be here now ~ with a Conscious Love Orgasm"
It's finding the balance but I'd rather be kissing you!
Yes I'm ready for all your flowing Inspiration Fantastic.
You will have to get promotion up to voluptuous Super muse #1.
That's what I DESIRE IS your vivacious pussy enraptured in delight,
your mouth devouring my cock as I bring you to another Orgasm.
Magical fountains crescendos with Goddess' honey nectar and bliss.
Your wild kisses sucking and lickin' ~ A small, tight, arse to die for!
The ecstasies in our union ~ tantric transcendence of all our senses,
all our feelings of Intimacy are consumed, you are lost in an erotic
dreamy Paradise; I'm deep inside you. Our 'Love With Lust' Tour.
Romantic hyper sensitive adventures, all tooled up, cum on over.
"Who invented the illusory arts of sensory Pleasure?"
Give me these, sweetness of life ~ not the insane evils!

"You can cum behind me"
"I fell in love with you when I saw you eat your Omelet"
"You can rub it anywhere just not on my face"
Freedom means it's Absolutely not Relatively FREE; No Offers!
Your mind is melting my Yoni with your lustful tongue, lips kisses;
Seducing the man. Honey moon of Acid bliss by the turquoise sea.
'I was looking for heavenly blowjobs under twinkly violet stars'
You wanna be wild inside me? I wanna be wild sat on top of you!
"I can slightly feel a bit of waviness ~" Sweet arse Your love
*poems touch my heart ~ Crystal Highs * erupting volcanoes.*

*

'Money Mania'
'They'd kill you in America!'
"Fucked off with all his dosh to Mecca!"
Out of his Mind on Benzo Fury!
"Never got my Lottery ticket, yu bastard!"
"Two hours in Rio had a gun to my head"
Beaten up left for dead ~ they all got robbed,
mugged by a load of 12 year olds for flip flops.
With big guns and nothing to lose. Bing, Bang!
One of 'em got battered! Fact of life ~ gotta go barefoot

*

The Standing Wave
"How does a heart ~ Open?"
'Wei Wu Wei' ~ 'Doing Not Doing'
'Just to be your TRUE ~ natural self'
Plasma Love frequency in crystal balls.
Big Sun grid work will melt us to Peace.
*Collapsing electro * magnetic duality into Zero.*
Time is in the dimension you put it ~ 5th 7th 9th.
Something new will be created ~ A spark!
Take the Pleasure of falling in One

PARADISE NOW

Traveling through a chimera ~ Invisible different dimension.
We're living in a Global reality today not Medieval Feudalism.
Experimental, more Creative ~ going with FREE SPIRITUAL
MAGICAL/HIGH TECH/ POETICAL/BEAUTY/FANTASTICAL
*ZERO POINT ENERGY FIELD * What's Time gotta do with it?*
Psychedelic Eyes of the future ~ in a moment of forever & ever.
Tuning into blissful Enlightenment not a Monster of your Mind!
Why do YOU have to own and conquer everything YOU see?
We are the Trance tribe ~ beautiful nymphs naked in a jungle
emphasising the amazing Power of nature's standing wave ~
*

"I'll take the Love Not the Slave"

Instinct ~ mesmerised on Victoria Vetri's sublimely, sexy furry bikini!
'A primitive tribeswoman escapes being sacrificed and goes on the
run hounded by hunters and flesh eating Dinosaurs' ~ Another
Prehistoric Adventure! Getting the women's vote was a massive
fantasy to achieve!
*

"Haven't seen a Lemon for five years"

Look at that he was down the mine ~ you spinning the wool for
blankets for our troops And they're playing croquet and Bridge!
You've ration coupons, they're drinking milk coffee. While you're
suffering with consumption they're knocking back the Brandies!
They had electricity while you were still burning wax candles!
They had hot baths while you had a tin bath by the kitchen fire,
and you carried the water from a rain barrel or the garden well.
Oh! There's our lads in uniform doing such a good job, being
sacrificed; Ultimately for King and HIS Realm! God bless 'em!
Had to empty a toilet into a lorry, they'd China cups and maids.
"Bless 'em all, bless 'em all, the long and the tall and the short"
The things men and women do in Life! "Come on lads get up,
out the trenches or I'll have to shoot you all!" ~ Bless 'em all.

<u>*P*assion Feast * Love Comet</u>
"Just because you licked my pussy ~
doesn't mean you can use my toothpaste too!"
'Goin' off like a fuckin Rocket that's what you make me do'
"You can watch me cum while I cook in my little dress".
"I see that you have the respect for me so that if I say
don't cum in my mouth you wont" ~ Tantric alignment.
Hot pussy muscles, "Would you like to cum into my body?"
"You're legally allowed to do what you want to do"
"And s/he's looking for Love in all the right places"
Lie down I'll put the kettle on ~ Where yu goin where yu been?
Dreams to release hidden lascivious feelings and emotional love.
Erotic Supernovas, Erotic Desires, Erotic waves ~ Cosmic juicy.
Are you wearing your sexy socks? Anticipation is off the scale!
Can't wait for the next kiss of your lips, sharing your exotic sexy
creativity ~ feeling your romantic tenderness, gently within mine.
Dissolving in her light ~ "All my Inspiration has come from You"
"I Love being ~ with you Inside me" ~ Wet inside for a blessing.
Do you like me sucking your erect clitoris, licking primal nectar?
I wanna be in that one eating your vibrant fertility, soaking bliss!
"Just because I keep having multiple Orgasms
doesn't mean I can go on forever…..STOP!"
*

<u>*'Love on the Rocks'*</u>
"Don't talk about that ~
not talkin' 'bout what we don't want,
talk about what we do want" ~ dripping Yoni.
Facing her pussy ~ starring right back at me.
Sexual secrets of an irresistible Pagan liaison.
Just sit it on it!

Welcome Home Goddess

You took me back to calm harmony of mind ~ that can be found.
Lots of amazing insights in the little things of life, sublime Kisses.
'Sucking your cock is sublime' WOW! 'Waking up with you, cum
*dripping like honey * and coffee too! YOU ARE A DELIGHT.*
Tell your puffy nipples to keep pert and hard like boiled eggs
they need to be sucked and your pussy juices spread like jam;
Tasty and sweet just like you ~ I want to lick your hot sweat.
We are partners in passion, desire, blow jobs and other jobs.
Thinking of the bliss on the end of your tongue ~ in your mouth,
reflected in your smiling, tender eyes. Your Love is Paradise ~
Your nature is Bliss and you are sharing it all with your Lover.
I'll enjoy ecstasies when your anticipation drives you too crazy
and you have to hunt me down. In the meantime keep wet and
full of desire for me and full of Universal INSPIRATION LOVER.
Your erotic messages are Amazing! Keep your PINK UNIVERSE
bubbling ~ inside your soaking rainforest. I See you as a water
nymph just risen out of the Cosmic foam, I'm cumming to you,
caressing your lemon breasts and we fuck forever, crescendos
under the Shiva moon. You dissolve back into the ocean ~ I fly
to our next assignation ~ your mouth guides me and I FILL IT.
*YOUR HEART * PERFECT BLISS * RAPTUROUS ORGASMS.*
KEEP FULL POWER & GET READY FOR LUSCIOUS KISSES.
Fantastic I feel so fulfilled and happy that you have these deep
feelings for me and for yourself, that I fill your hunger especially
for the nice things. Need the delightful pleasure of your Bindaas.
Where are you sunbeam? Looking forward to seeing you, holding
you, kissing you, being naked with you. I'm waiting for you with
a very happy heart. Take the Super deliciously sweet Express.
"I'll go anywhere with you for your pony ride." "Am I the pony?"
You're my pony, I call you Divine ~ Rain or shine.

'Guwahati, Assam'. Guardian p14. 16/7/2012
'Indians have expressed horror at video footage of a teenage
girl being sexually assaulted by a laughing mob of more than
twelve men in a busy street outside a bar in NE India. No one
intervened for up to 45 minutes during the attack which was
filmed by an off duty journalist and a cameraman from News-
Live channel. The footage was broadcast on news channels
prompting a debate on women's safety in India and asked why
the journalists didn't intervene. Police have been criticized
over their initial indifference towards the attack which
took place just minutes from the nearest Police station!
The attack has highlighted the dangers of being a woman
in India. A global poll last month voted India the worst G20
country for women, behind even Saudi Arabia. India's national
commission for women said the teenage victim had been
treated like an animal and had cigarette burns all over her body'
This is another example of the grotesque treatment of women.
A woman executed by the Taliban for adultery, put on internet!
There's long lists of inhumane treatment of women, of so called
'honor killings' to forced marriages of teenage girls in Pakistan
to the Qatif girl who was gang raped but ordered by a court in
Saudia Arabia to be given 200 lashes for the crime of 'mingling'
A Christian girl was framed by a Moslem imam for burning pages
of the Koran for which the penalty is death! Even more barbaric
examples are the mass raping of Moslem women, estimated to be
20,000, as a militarily condoned 'objective' during the horrendous
1990's fascist war in Bosnia and the sex slave and torture prisons!
Headlines: Another massacre of civilians including children,
taken off the bus in Houla, Syria, shot dead ~ as seen on TV!
'So little can be done against the carnage' an eye witness said.
A new massacre, 13 workers found, ashes in a fertiliser factory.

SEXY * ENCHANTMENT

Booked in room 36 waiting for your manifestation to arrive.
PANTING for your smoldering love ~ Hieros Gamos on time.
Anticipation of sucking your throbbing nipples and clitoris!
Walking in a lush green meadow long grass full of buttercups.
I'll have an extra Juicy Jelly Delight with Vulva cream sauce.
Steaming, hot, spicy and wet. Your divine specialty beginning
to bubble with desire. To be invited into the Inner Love Temple
of a Goddess, to kiss the lips of an angel, caress the big breasts
of such a gorgeous woman, to be given delicious blisses going
together deep into the magical dimension of Spiritual Passion.
THANK YOU I think you've brought a new Geisha concept into
the Modern world. It has a lot of sharing ~ Pure tantric pleasure
trip to enjoy which is always delightful with You and I also have
a ravishing Concubine who loves a lager shandy & cheesecake!
*Wow! filled with blessings of a Love Goddess, I AM * Thank you.*
Now Multi dimensionally * 2b 2gether when r u 3 next 4 Bliss ~*

*

Natural Lagoon

*The depth of our body mind Spirit * bliss connection Amazes me.*
Sitting on a deserted white sandy beach, the water fabulously
warm, soft, fresh air on my skin, so relaxing I love it ~ the jungle
comes right up to the lapping sea ~ You can feel Pachamama
Alive breathing ~ YOU are the Only other one in this Eden.
Our communication transcends all the bullshit and fears ~
We love the same cake and Love the pleasure of each other.
I always honour your Goddess ~ took a trip down her river.
Now in a surreal donut shop. Looking for some cherry jelly
for your divine purring pussy to devour. Anticipation of ~
*A Super summer enjoying your sun * beams flooding through*
the clouds. Call me when you are dripping on fire with desire.

Moon Glade *Angelic Cake

Enhanced suckulent specialist gently caress my lips & breasts
You are a Fucking genius, "I'm dripping just thinking of you"
I'm missing you deliriously ~ I Love you with all my passion!
'Beautiful your spirit is in my heart ~ my spirit is in your heart'
Everything pumping, your love is Rocket fuel taking me to Venus.
Yearning for you ~ burning me up like an exploding Supra Nova
*

Virtuous Intention

Dispelling all her fears for a promise of Love.
She's a virgin widow ~ married in her infancy.
Her husband died before she arrived at puberty.
Doing the sacrifices, morning, noon and night.
Living devoted to her man ~ natural affection.
Thrusting from on top, writhing up and down.
Sucking in deep a delicious, sweet mango fruit.
Holding his hard, throbbing lingham in her hand,
pressing between her lips ~ moving it in her mouth.
Touching her tongue everywhere swallowing it to the very end!
Without hesitation entering ~ back and forth between her thighs.
*

'In Godless They Trust'

Nothing real in that, no ground to perceive the truth, faith, reality.
'As a clear lake ~ a clear mind gives a clear reflection before it'
Loving a bit of devotion on her smoldering lips, no doubt about it.
Who has any morals? What is 'prurient' to an Open Mind/heart?
'Evil to him who evil thinks' "I'm not gonna hurt you ~ for now"
Are you happy, do you feel inspired, do you love life's beauty?
Act according to your Inclination ~ Imagination > subconscious.
"I'm in the Sunny tribe, You feel so much to me INSIDE"
Mindful ~ Mindless, Don't be attached ~ to manifestation.

Her Sun Worshipper
At least Jesus wasn't a Mason ~ "he's a little sweetheart!"
"They'd come ~ rape your wife, take your TV, then yur fucked!"
More hooligans, surrounded on all sides by Idiots - one channel!
Barbaric the things he did to get 'Post Traumatic Stress'
Black Daleks on a Rampage ~ smoldering crimson pussy's lips!
As soon as she walked into the Hotel the Alarm would go off!
Beheaded that afternoon!

*

'She's Full of Love'
Your Intent Is Our Reality ~ Love Is Feeling, Is Life.
Love mixed with Passion brings you closer to the Divine.
We're all equal under the Sun ~ sharing its Cosmic radiance.
In the All In One then You are Free.
I'm in the Love ~ letting go
of her smokin' hips!

*

Bonding Visionary Plants
"Love Is An Energy Out of Light ~ flowing essence"
He was a mirror vendor from Machu Pichu, Peru.
With an Index of Psyche*active drug compounds.
His wife's got CIA. drones flying over her house.
Feeding the Programs with our own thoughts.
"She's got 'Insatiable' tattooed on her lips"
'Live Simply So That Others May Simply Live'
"Tried to make it work but they're totally bonkers"
They're Satanic travelers and not any friends of mine
who were escaping from a decapitation of the Medina's ~
Revenge for those whipped and tortured under Holy laws!
& what this says about Pleasure & Pain?
"Fuck that!"... circling Predatory Birdy.

<u>D</u>eeper & deeper loving
"Drugs, Sex, Rock & Roll, they don't come here for swimming"
Dripping Passion * feeling Hot liquid ~ honey smooth.
You are a sparkling Cocoon beside the waters edge ~
A beautiful sensation inside, your sweet erotic temple.
I loved your poem ~ gliding in light consciousness.
It's a gift falling into your open arms,
it's a gift falling into your caresses.
Enjoy the revolution ~ experience the love, be happy.
Your soft kisses alight on my lips ~ blisses floating
through kaleidoscopic air from your body to mine.
Cool them in a bucket of cold water or tie them to a Cosmic kite
to fly to the end of the sky. Hold on tight! What you doing later?
I got the limes, sensual jelly and fruity condoms; Anything else?
Is there a white star shining brightly outside your front door?
I can feel it, sweetly delicious. What's cooking gorgeous?
"I'm at home, why not stop by for a kiss?"
*

<u>Wanting to feel your lips and kisses</u>
Am I your muse? Loving your poems, love your passion, love
your arse, love your beans and mash, love to be in your mouth,
love to caress your purring pussy. Where's your light shining?
Missed sharing a lemon cake with my super sexy Tantaliser.
I kiss your lips, I lick your soft wet Yoni full of lustful desires.
I caress your hard nipples pulsating hot, feverish joyfulness.
I cum deep into your thrusting hips, filling your senses with bliss.
You fill my melting body, mind & spirit with exquisite Happiness.
We are on a Cosmic journey sharing our mutual attractiveness.
You're falling to bits, a breakthrough! How does your heart feel?
I'm holding your hand in mine ~ my delicate inspiration.
Cumming all over you, on top, behind, under, inside you.

Multi * Cellular
In our Custody Suites!
Took a Venus Rocket ~
'Given Plasma energy to free us here today'
Not Controls to Enslave us Mr. President.
Our Solar Activation furnace burning light.
IN YOU
*

Bankster Terrorism Rigged The System

Why would anyone ever want to use weapons against another life?
Ask at the Bank for International Settlements. Where's that Lucifer?
Ask the Corporatcrazy, ask despotic creatures from Jekyll Island.
Don't ask the Debt slaves they don't have a F.....g clue!
Internal Revenue being heisted, endemic Insider Trading.
"No Government Agency can Overrule the Federal Reserve"
That can't be True can it? How about for Criminal Actions?
Quick to prosecute those for stealing a loaf and flat screen TV;
in a riot but not the Dynasties inflicting a Meltdown on people!
They're parasites with horrendous tapeworms eating it all up.
Robbed through Inflation, need 20 million kip for a bio yoghurt.
This fascist Monopoly backed up by all its Government Forces.
Creating money/debt out of thin air like a magician's rabbit.
'World's richest 2% own more than 50% of Global assets.
In the US richest 10% control 90% + of the Wealth!' Why?
What's that tell you and who owns the busted banks & what now?
Bankrupted society & scooped it ALL up! We've bailed them out!
Manipulating the Business Cycles, interest up, less $ circulating.
The Economy is Crashing you're losing your Home tonight mate!
Desperately needs a job on an Opium clipper ship to Shanghai.
And who wants to Pillage a neighboring country? Make a queue!
"It's all about being True ~ to Yourself"

Toucan Inspiration
"If you can't be happy without ~ then you can't be happy with"
If you live in a shed and you have Peace of Mind then it wouldn't
matter if you're in a mansion. If you're living in a mansion and it
won't give you peace of mind then it's no good being in a mansion.
*
Kali's Kiss
"Eat me, I don't give a fuck, I'll get another one"
"1980's the last time I painted ~ the skirting boards!"
"There's a level ~ you cross it, then you're in Fairyland"
Going backwards ~ Forwards, passing on the LOVE & LIGHT.
Without doubt, lots & lots of bliss ~ Visualisation in meditation.
A Light worker's manifestation
*
Bread Strikes & Disposable Gold Plates
'Truth' never changes ~ Truth is always changing! Gulf streams.
Enjoying new freedoms, neighbors brought back a black slave!
Landscape's colours expressing the psychological state of Mind
Many people can't sense the energies in Abstract Expressionism.
Leaving the 'Meaning' OPEN ~ enjoy real places, real sunshine.
'Brush strokes, new language conveying new sensations'.
Feeling the Spirit of the Revolution ~ not of the Emperor.
Speaking to the emotions of the luminous heart.
*Interactions of Life's * luminescence*
*
Breaking the Taboos!
House of Pleasure, house of Heaven, Temples of Hieros Gamos.
New rhythms, mining a vein of MDMA, best place on the Planet.
Milky way organisms, energetic subconscious of spinning mass.
*Psychic * Magic * Mercury zooming through your empty brain.*
"Music should be Free ~Juicy spirit" playing Cosmic Infinity.

In Purdah Not Lithe
'That experience is not allowed to be felt'
'Feel Joy not kill Joy!' A different view.
Reverse Psychology or Juicy Passion?
"I'm a sinuous Erotic Surrealist" in bliss
with you ~ I like you to slide in and out easily.
Cuming with the flow ~ Orgasms on the beach,
wet sexual caresses in the warm lapping waves.
Kissing her hard nipples feeling her body's ripples.

*

Lips in the Night Sky
Puja is prayer, a good fuck, orgasms of cuming closer to God.
"Love mixed with Passion brings you closer to the Divine"
"When I was between wives ~ being out on the Rampage!"
She made me so happy ~ I just want her to be happy too.
"Are you a dancer?" "I can dance ~ living in progressive Trance"
'I'm gettin a blow job And I'm getting a nice hard cock in my pussy!'
Sucking blisses, exploding sex swept through lust's delirious vortices.
Psychedelic Moonbeams in an ancient forest on black silk sheets.
Full of glistening alchemy and magic setting man and woman free.

*

Different View
"How can anyone take themselves seriously ~ when there's so
much Junk orbiting in our Minds which is only a Big Illusion"
"What made that damage?" 'A Fool's Missile', Who is guilty?
"You don't feel any Pain, you just stop breathing"~ way to go!
Sacred woods, destroying it for profit, missing its whole magic.
"Diabolical but accepting it comes from their Totalitarianism"
Shiva changes every second ~ destroys Worlds every breath in ~
every breath out...TIME ~ where's the Holy Roman Empire now?
'Seeing it as a Source not a Resource' Father Time ~ Mother Space

Be In Oneness
Holding it in the fire of Illusion
By being fully in the moment….
The Higher Will working thru the Lower ~
You are the vehicle for manifesting it.
Soul consciousness is the All in One ~ "She's different"
"If we don't give the Form they have nothing to Fill in"
Remembering not to go into the comparison trip.
What do you think Sexy Angel?
*

Power in your Pussy's Crème Delice
Making their own De*light ~ psychedelicate skinful.
Sending probes… Does an octopus have a brain?
In your Cosmic DNA. program working in every cell.
Colours of a chemical Chameleon, of Flora's flowers.
Sperm surviving to impregnate your fertile embryos.
Too many Robins are flocking in the orchard ~
laying eggs. Birds don't have dramas do they?
It's like a live butterfly collection in there!
Creepy crawlies filling in all the space gaps.
Organic balance ~ "Put the bacon on Love!"
*

Start the Automatic Flow
Experiment to build the Castle in different shapes.
Melting point of all the Star systems in all galaxies.
Lotuses blooming out of the muddy, gravity of Mind.
Who has a Mental Problem? Ask a Think Tank of the Heart.
Love energy falling on the whole atmosphere with soft petals.
The authentic Source ~ A Sustainable living vision of delight.
Famous for being non organised, non BIO>Organic.
It's Not Rocket science ~ Ask the Dragon dreamers!

Super Jumpy
Jumped out of the loop ~
Breaking the laws of karma.
Into the clear space ~ reflecting dhamma.
"When you get to where you're going
you wont need the signposts anymore".
They don't know ~ no one knows.
You know things you don't even know!
"leave your ego at the door"
Who are these people?

*

Sunbathing Baba vis a vis Grand Holy Regimental Censorship!
'You're Free' ~ to follow the rules, the orders, the Regs; By-Laws!
Why ~ at whose behest is this moral code of Authority enforced?
'Life's not a formula all conforming to the same value pattern'
Real expression of your thoughts, ideas, speech, to remain free,
to become self ~ realised; 'Why am I different?' A true Catalyst
for Understanding the rest. Who is this Subject's character?
Let's please have some mercy! Met him in the Psyche ward.
Met her meditating, chanting, naked in love at Omkareshwar

*

'Burnout Man'
It's all a dream your Mind is creating for your*self each instant.
Disciplined to be Happy ~ Everlasting Lust ~ Light hearted.
'Don't want to, can't live up to other people's expectations'
Girls with sparkling eyes ~ Love you share the same feeling.
The wave hits the beach ~ 'I'm happy to have this moment'.
Utopian dream living inside a sublime, Bottichelli melody.
He's on a mission ~ doing it on the river, sinking or swims.
A Citizen of Earth; Survived in an Igloo, Glasgow in June.
"If I find you lovely do I love you?"

Milky Way * Supernova
"If I don't own it I don't have it"
"What you do is who you are"
Finding is when you don't look anymore.
Cherry Lip Balm ~ Eccentric Accepted.
"If she empty she ain't curly"
Kali Sisters of the Shakti tribe
*

Two Suns
Energetic Shot ~ Oriental Magic.
Beauty unravels, drink the nectar.
Spreadin' it out to all light workers.
'Existential Fear' ~ Lips to lips, hips to hips,
blisses, kisses ~ nearly fucking burnt my mouth!
The Orbs are coming ~ All the Indigo children.
"I'm coming inside me just being inside you"
Light bodies melting in you.
Frequency of a Star system.
Jupiter's passion is enflamed!
*

Other Skulls & Crossbones
"We're the Fun Loving Pirates"
"We're goin' in mate" ~ Overt not covert convert!
We're not supposed to be there ~ we are there, giggling!
"I'm trashed in the Green fields; Will somebody Please
come and get me; That's when I got a mobile phone!"
Space creates, She pervades all ~ while Time destroys.
Shiva changes every second ~ every breath out, every breath in.
Ma Kali's cup is never empty ~ drops of blood, holding Man's
ugly false Ego * Nature cuts it off in one go. Garlands of heads;
Infinite rebirths ~ around the neck of a playful 16 year old girl.
She was in touch with the tip of Shiva's tongue.

Sparkling Sprites

Living out the details of a Elementals tale.
Mermaids ~ you're in tune with free spirit.
Creative with the life ~ perfectly balanced.
Nature's Spiral Consciousness ~ unbound
dancing under the stars at night by myself.
Getting in the rhythm ~ Do whatever you want.
Manifest what you want, your dreams coming true!
Went to the Pixie park, you made me a charm bracelet.
"Teach me what I've got to learn today"
"I was really magical when I was 18"
*Angel dreams of angel wings * fairy daughter*

*

Good to Know

If you see it like that it'll be like that ~ Watch the Fear & paranoia!
Fantasies of unhappy arranged wives, who do you want to be Priya?
Siddhis giving you powers, captivating Apsaras for their Pleasures.
Not even Earth women they're Celestial beings,
more than eager for you to leave your body.
Beachfront on Venus with Rati full of desire.
Maya in super heat ~ Sex is the Sun on fire.
What an amazing beauty she is!
"Adam forgot God on the G spot!"
His five senses became his Master ~ Kamdev.
Eros riding the serpent igniting all passions.

*

Questioning things

Thoth don't look back! Who wants to turn into salt crystals?
When you choose Rules, Rights, laws and Regulations.
Their aim is ~ to make the Highest profit at auction.
Tripping on my own inside the tomb of a Pharaoh.
Meditating on ~ 'Loving It' ~ Exactly..

Shocks And Awes!
'The Final air campaign' "I take my orders only from him!"
Bombed the city of Hanoi over 11 days, Christmas 1972.
120 B52s and 100 other Bombers in an evil, Genocidal Blitz!
Sky on fire, burning bright red, Earth trembling back & forth!
In that carnage if that's not a Crime Against Humanity what is?
150,000 US soldiers died; 2 million Vietnamese & 4 million wounded.
Same Strategy as using in Iraq, the killing technology's got better!
What justification can people have to destroy another like this?

*

Psyche delicate Picnic.
With Party Girl ~ "forever One more!"
"You got Champagne, you got Ego, Cocaine!"
You got hash you got cash, an exotic STD. rash!
How many people took MDMA and raped someone?
Alcohol is that fuel ~ try some Yoga & tantric dreaming.
Hearing the rhythm of the beat ~ I pulled the spears out!
Blending it all together ~ not very far from super carnal!
Consciously outta yu head ~ yu is in this moment

*

I Never said that!
"You can have too much of a good thing" 12 orgasms in a row!
'Temple slaves often performing a lot of religious prostitution'
"I'd rather give up food than passion!" I love your slinky hips.
"How many times I said in my head, I want you to Kiss me ~"
Something to put in the mind getting more passionate every day!
Keeping a commitment; I don't want to have to break a promise!
Tuned to your frequency ~ chakras opened, blazing Pussy on fire!
"Isn't it amazing we found each other?" Dreaming of you in Awe.
Breaking the rules of love ~ Free spirits entwined in deep roots.

Turning damp

The Queen tried using a State poverty Fund to heat her Palaces!
It won't rain all weekend, some sunny spells! Should brighten
up later, getting blustery. Grey start and it will be more windy.
Amber alert as we head into Monday. Coldest summer in 18 yrs.
Balmy end to September with a 11% fewer butterflies forecast.
Some say Carbon Emissions is just to Impose a new Green Tax

*

Easy Tiger!

Pint of Coke Please; Those very 'Private Collections'
'More Tigers in captivity in US. than exist in the wild!
That cretin, he worked that bad karma out on you!
In a relationship with a lover ~ that's Togetherness
not Dependency ~ Love without any responsibility!
Depends what context, how Attached to it you are.
Not having the flow, have to let it go ~ in Compassion.
Why have ½ when you can have a whole? Slave market!
It's ALL Cosmic & Chemically ~ Multi * dimensionality.
Let the Neutrinos do it ~ I do believe in hot fusion's mix.
Dance Is An Art ~ Music is an Art ~ being in the moment.
Isometric, diametric showed me I can have altered states
of Conscious, losing the states of Ego's gravity ~ No fear
of death as I feel like I've lived a good, full life, Free!
"Real Zouk is in evolving not hierarchical static rules"
We're on the peak of the curve ~ surfing light.
'Patriotism it's not enough I must have
no hatred or bitterness for Anyone'

*

Suspended Animation.

'A Lesbian went to weight watchers for velvet Aficionados.
"You are what you eat" ~ "What, you callin' me a cunt!?"
"We Celebrate our Magic Cake, joints and chocolate bombs!"

'In her eyes'

"We come from another Star ~ we are the Resident Aliens here!"
Came of our free will to live in this gravity. It's y/our Creation
don't have to look for the outcome ~ Stay in your Truth, live it!
Everyone is allowed to be different no right or wrong judgment.
It's just You and we find ourselves and see the dramas we make,
carry around. See it as a Process ~ becoming in the Sensitivity.
To have it not run away from it, no one to judge you; Only you.
Andromeda's knocked out all the Nuclear, fell into its frequencies
'They want your Free will ~ to channel us light to save the Planet'
Some like healing with colour & sound waves of the White Dragons.
You have to ask for it, 'Please, please, Missiles disintegrate, Amen!'
They're cleaning up ~ Chemical vapour trails, for the last 20 years.
Others are transforming energy into Plasma balls on Aquarius ~.
At the last census sixteen cities are on the dark side of the Moon.
Time is non linear ~ allow yourself to dream and Thank You.
Letting your 'Imagination' run through your creative potential.
*

Moving On with Eanna

Just took me to the border of Delta crossing into Theta ~
Operating in the awareness ~ brain waves calmed down.
No technique ~ follow the flow, diving in with closed eyes.
Visiting the Arambol Mental Hospital for Spiritual people.
South Anjuna for dance therapy ~ just keep movin' in trance.
The protocols of remote viewing ~ hooked in lucid dreaming.
Trying to disconnect you from the Nature of yourself.
"Knowing what it is after DMT. reduced me to tears!"
Communicating with our Creator ~ we are souls.
"I said to Jesus, oh please ~ give me a chance"
On the journey 'let the dead bury the dead'
The divine stopped me, said you're off in the wrong dimension.
"Old time relationships are over ~ now in Love with it all"

Saraswati's Friend

The infidel Vedas, not God's chosen ones, would only spook them!
"Krishna always is the now" ~ You're just watching the movie.
*Not taking it **P**ersonally so not feeling the attachment of **P**ain.*
Our attention gets caught up by the 'Objects' of desire's duality.
Being Formless ~ serene, divine, sublime Identityless' caress.
Knowing subconsciously ~ through hypnotic trance, Tummo.
Meeting a Master of Tratak, getting the concept of Pranayam!
Look into his eye once and you swoon in ecstasy with him.
After he spoke people fell in irresistible bliss ~
When he gives you his Mala you fall in love.

*

Sirius Orchids

Lifting the Veil, the ringing in your ears, shows you're alive.
Falling in the emptiness; Melody is what brings it all together.
From duality to multi * dimensionality ~ Opening up your brain.
Unconscious Forces ~ met a very pretty coquettish Existentialist.
Saw rainbows reflecting off the tips of her eyelashes in sunlight.
Never knowing the Evolving ~ Ignorance of an Extinctentialist.
'Fluidity ~ so as not to limit the viewer's response'

**

Tower of Burj El Mur, Beirut, only ever used as a sniper outpost.
Memorial to inhumane Internal conflict ~ Dominating the Skyline!
Array of images derived from the unconscious are superimposed.
"What's his name?" "I don't have any idea!" Tribe's in revolt ~
Mr. Simply Naïve; It means they lied! They don't think like us.
*Random, indeterminate **S**ymbols. Who Fired First? 'Inshallah!'*
"I'll buy this house and make it a Communication Centre"
200 types of Roses in the garden igniting Jupiter's moon
then 20 to 30 Killer Whale pods swam by ~
Beautiful smile ~ beautiful light inside.

Constructed Whatever!

Never know how things happen; Principles how they're existing.
Are you really ever ready? Take your Mind off it. Relax in bliss.
They'll try to fulfill your wish, simple Advaita Vedanta fishermen.
Bow down to Ma Kali & let it happen ~ accept your Cosmic kiss.
She takes everything and eats it all up for the best.
She should always be the Queen ~ of contradictions.
Being it rather than doing it…..

*

Tattoo Projectionist

You fell into her eyes ~ Maya Kaliskya coming (from Moscow).
Maybe she's got an overactive pussy, gave her a Pill of light.
When you smell her you'll get enflamed ~ "You are Enflamed!"
Representing Jupiter's Magnificence, holding up the Front line.
"For the best of me #1 and for all the other #1's too."
Sometimes you don't even know what's the best for
You and you only see it when you've gone 3 corners!
You believe in what you wish to happen. Opening ~
"It's a mad game out there ~ but who really cares?"
All of a sudden you're there if you don't get distracted.
What a beautiful iridescent blue on her sculptured back!
"They love to get you & you love to be got"
"Touching her perfect body with your Mind"

*

Shakti * Pachamama

Kali is SPACE;
Without it where would God be in Cosmic time?
Girls who make LIFE ~ holding up the POWER.
Girls who have tantrums in Tantric energy fields.
Here is Seven Billion versions of Planet EARTH.
Your choice ~ the Epic path of life to Nirvana.
*Mysticism*absolute no boundaries ~ Full Spacey*

Levers of Power

Controlling the Monetary System ~ financial flow, life stream!
Controlling so called democracies & their 'National Interests'
Controlling all the Governments & insatiable Corporations, P2;
Controlling the Illuminati's Gold Houses, Vatican holy Assassins.
Knights of Malta sitting in the Royal box at the Coliseum.
Now reflecting it through the reality of our multi * strand DNA.
Feeling it all ~ responding to Truth, harmonic convergence.
Who's working only for those type of Demons?
The Dragons in retreat, fighting a guerilla war!
We're through our Star gate, we're in the NEW.
The less we Identify with it ~ the more we Allow for SPACE.
To be Open to receive ~ to hold it up in us, to own its sense.
Have No attachment, letting go ~ tuning that new frequence.
Clear channelings coming from Omnigalactic beams of Light.

*

'Self - Imposed Crisis'

"Has to Happen in each moment"
Living here Unfolding in the Silence watching everything turn ~
Calling all Angels to come in ~ making an Army of Light Force.
Bring it over the internet frequency 'This is Still*Free for everyone'

*

Dark Vedas

Old Masters of Planet Ratsnake.
New energies of light & sound ~
Being Open to it ~ Space Maker
Giving us the Positive purpose.
Why nature changes it ~ simply Wonderful.
Shit happens by itself and falls on your head!
Not to mention a 5 * Megaton Phosphor bomb
dropped on you by a country you don't even know.
Yet they disintegrated the lot in your village! Why?
& all they felt was a shudder in their Stealthy wings!

97

Tools ~ 72 Channels!
Feeding us all the Negativities.
Nice wallpaper in your own box.
Otherwise how can you let go ~
it catches you at the next corner.
We're living in the energetic moment ~ he understood
we have all the time to let go ~ coming to Zero point space.
You would only lay down and relax in the arms of the woman.
"Can participate like everyone else but not to Dominate"
"Normally you cook with Love and everything is Tasty!"
'Her lips are full blooded!'
She could see you had some Shiva in you.
Spark of Individual fire ~ lighting up!
*

It's a Concept:
That's her beauty, her amazing gorgeous arse and she knows it!
I'm sure she does things she can't talk about ~ Tickling her ribs!
Going through the flames, Empowering & the embodiment of it ~
There's your List, now go & fuckin' do it! Some people like that!
Going with the flow ~ can't say I'll be home for dinner darling.
I gave her all the allowance to change my dreams.
Yeah, she can really hold up the Centre of Attention!
I want to make a Tantric Temple, creating, making beauty.
This fruit is growing by itself ~ love takes time to blossom.
Cultivating loving kindness ~ In a Paradise of Earth.
"You're a sexy piece of crumpet from Venus oozing jelly jam"
*

Faith Is Truth
"I'm happily in Love at the minute" ~ Allowing Trust to Trust.
It's only the ignorant and fearful who hide, ridicule, suppress,
Censor it, made it sinful for revealing our human beauty! Why?

Was it natural to nature?
"Why should we save you when you're murdering each other?"
Hooked in the comfort, material zone of a Platinum, Gold Visa.
Can't hold the higher frequencies ~ draining their life force.
"The King is dead ~ Long live the King" not fucking again!
Switching one mutation with another ~ from the same virus.
Speaking every hypocrisy never allowed to say the Truth ~
Feeling energy is in-between the words ~ Silent Spaces.
"I'm like on liquid magic mushrooms in the flow ~ of Love"
Taking your position in the Net work and working with them.
They all want to show the veil and see what's beyond it.
The old matrix dimension ~ conditionings into the new.
It's about Freedom ~ saying the Truth in all sorts of ways.
Projecting your visions of Cosmic vitality, beauty and purity.
Coming from the base of simply being honest to human nature.
Integral * Quintessence ~ tuned into Sunshine receiving Divine.

*

Higher * Best * Light
"You only see them if you make Space for them"
In direct Alignment with the Galactic centre ~
Christ consciousness spinning in Free Orbit.
We're at Zero Point energy 00000000000'
Putting the clock back to 'Full of Love'
Have to let go ~ getting a reflection
Discernment ~ becoming a reality

*

Love Tart
High on Life ~ light dreamer.
"Who's gonna let my children starve?"
"When that laptop dies what am I gonna do?"
Tasting her Love Buttons on my tongue!
"You're a surreal supra multi orgasmic fuck"

Mouth Congress

Seduction, swollen breasts, amorous possibilities kindling desire.
Person beloved enflaming his lustful passion on a moonlit night.
Intention filled with Intoxicating Love and respect for a Goddess.
Have direct experience of the jungle ~ recognizing my relations.
'Your Intent is to make nature happen'
"For Love does not care for time or order"
Visible and erect in the embrace of thighs.
This is how I want my Rock & Roll to be!
*

Subjective * Objective * Separation.

Low speed naked sunbathing Yoga on her roof. But it's not you!
A trick pulled on humanity, actions of the diabolical Straw man.
Fundamentally super constructed Hoax of Matrix conditioning.
You created delusional fields of Maya; Made us fearful, gave us
blame, shame, what you believe we're not allowed to do wrong!
*Mother Earth Is ~Trans*mutter of nature Channeling her energy.*
Realising the manifestation of Outside is Secondary. Primarily ~
*It's an Inner Process * living life. Try some gratitude & devotion.*
Day & night, dark & light, You're a Conqueror & the Conquered.
How all polarity is constructed for our own Self's Identifications.
*Giving & taking duality ~ Reality * Prana is existing all the time.*
The Controllers want you to hold on to somethin' that's no more.
Let go ~ feel holistic Universes' eternal Space ~Unity of Oneness
*

Spelling Mistake

'Vulva' …thinks it's a Volvo!
'You can put that in 4th and
cruise down the midnight highway'
You're coming up with gems.
We need to get the cherry jelly.
A few people came with wild fiori.

Coup de foudre Impressions
The woman full of devotion for her husband.
No sooner saw her than he fell in lust with her.
Thinking day and night of nothing but (possessing) her.
Ask Ravana about ruinous desires of enjoying the wives of others!
Nails scratching on her neck, breasts, thighs, back, stomach, legs.
Bending her body over his ~ Greatly enamored with each other!
Enjoying my love making, the bliss, pressing, natural juiciness.
In the light of that awareness
*
Always looking for the Spooks!
They did their special ceremony swimming free like fish in a prison.
Believing in Voodoo, witchcraft, desensitizing us all to Horror?
Another massacre on the street, it's all about V I O L E N C E !
Shot, Injured, maimed never gonna be the same again! Empathy!
Collateral damage, spinning excuses for crimes against humanity.
You have been brainwashed so you accept the most brutalised acts
known to mankind. It is legalized by regimes of Lucifer on you.
A frenzy of sharks feeding in the pond ~ like living in Hell.
Wipes people out, shooting anything that moves mentality!
Do you think they should spend $3 trillion on weapons?
Going to war ~ is that the future for our children?
Even goin' for water you're gonna get killed!
Mugging the people, awarded an inflationary 45 p. rise!
We're all economic slaves, some are happy to pay for it.
Most of us not realizing what is ~ The rest is all nature.
Becoming more conscious now that the President lies.
Living in a Criminal Justice System.
Royally fuckin' over the population.
Democracy is only a name ~
So is Indiscriminate Murder

HAARPie's!

They put a Sound Wave into the Cabals' under Earth caverns.
They had to run for it and exploded to bits inside New Babylon!
Lots of Peace Not War coming there, not wanting to Kill You!
Andromeda's Jedi warriors doing that; Stopping the Control &
Enslavement by the Machines, dominating us over 5000 years!
Remembering this again, getting it all back not the Dense Form.
Suddenly everyone had a Flash and we made it ~ transmuted it.
Gales into a tsunami ~ building up the internet psychic channels.
12 Zillion DNA strings on the way with lots of Funky monkey.

*

"Just Be Cool"

Four floors of whores at the Orchard Towers. Bless them all ~
They're all that good wherever they come from, essence of the sea.
Eating my oysters at the Pussy Bar each tasting like salty Sashimi
Legs spread, sitting on my face, tongue tip licking her velvet labia.
"Is that Spiritual?" Milarepa jumping out of the glass Twin Towers!
Stepped out of things, I don't Mind what's happening, 'Inshallah'
Cosmic sub consciousness is the most Important ~ Mind's mostly
Illusory unconscious ~ Bad vibes with his Reptiles! Wake up time!
Whatever happens, Space is Energy everywhere ~ Holistic You.
"The bad girls drink alcohol, good girls give happy Tantric fellatio"
Everyone living their own path ~ consciously not judge mentally.

*

Sunshine Heart

Energy field of feeling ~ seeing through opaque matter.
No more the invisible puzzle observing the Big picture.
Giving myself Space of ALLOWANCE for it to unfold ~
Light worker being aware and holding the presence in you.
Standing in your own shoes ~ taking it on and owning it.
Christ Love Consciousness ~ where we all come from.

FREE & EASY

Gone on a trip to his psychedelic Mecca of LSD.
Psyche's Limitless ~ boundless, eternal, affinity.
'Spiritual Awakenings' 'Within you without you'
"The process of learning has not to be learned"
Perspective ~ maintaining your own Integrity.
"One's own impulse of individuality, one's own rhythm, mantra
of the resonating sound ~ letting your mind take off to bliss"

*

Faiyum's Rose * Triton's Heart

Who is venerating intimacy and sensuality perfectly?
"She's delicate, beautiful, impressive, original, emotional,
intriguing to see what treasures are resonating within"
Hold onto your imagination ~ Adorable, brilliant Goddess.
Embracing your fragrances, sinuous, lithe, sparkling gems.
Particles of gold ~ changing the light effects to translucence.
Stunning, luxurious, kissing your dazzling, loosely flowing hair.
Passionately caressing her extravagantly dripping wet fighetta.
Super gorgeous senses of profusion, rampant fertility in rapture,
bursting flora, vital, raw, vigorous, pulsating, large magical lingam.
It's here to be Loved

*

"I'm the Sunshine Story"

"Your Heart Wants You ~ To Live In The Now"
Look after your being ~ Don't abuse yourself!
"When you have nothing ~ You have You"
Let your Imagination run ~ feeling Abstract creativity.
Not the logical Mind of control ~ being more dreamy.
Spontaneous Intertwine, I am a Free Spirit
depicting the JOYS of physical Love.
'Turning rain to rainbows'

This Is My Body ~ My Tantric Temple ~ 'Ignorance Is Violence!'
This book is dedicated to all women who have suffered sexual
violence, aggression, threat, intimidation, torture and atrocity!
'An estimated 20,000 Bosnian Muslim women were raped and
used as sex slaves' ~ 'Rape was/is being used as a weapon of war'
These men are using their primal instincts to behave in bestial ways.
Their need to prove their Power and dominance is taking over any
humanity they have and inflicting catastrophic trauma on women
and their families. Hierarchical, closed, feudal, warring, corrupted
cultures where a patriarchal system is sustained allowing for male
superiority yet not allowing them the freedom to treat women as
equal in any loving way. The laws & customs of misogynic societies
condone exploitation of women (and children) allowing males the
right to commit such horrendous crimes. Natural powers of sexual
attraction, of desire, of lust, unless the energies are channeled in a
free, mutually loving way where 'The Greatest Pleasure Is to Give
Pleasure' they become frustrated, angry, perverted and diabolical
without any respect! Freedom is to give and receive ~ Happiness.
Where these feelings of consensual love are freely shared the acts
of sex are able to give the couple a heightened awareness of bliss.
Where these feelings are not expressed but repressed, suppressed,
oppressed, depressed, the disconnect from reality brings psychosis.
Passion flows openly with Consciousness, being Unconditional Love.

'Eve-Teasing to War Booty!' 'Protect The Girls Now!' 16/12/2012
'A young student was gang raped & tortured by six men, thrown
from a moving bus & dumped naked on the streets of New Delhi.
She was so badly beaten with an iron bar her intestines had
to be removed. She remained in a critical condition in a coma
due to the trauma and serious injuries; Severe Organ Failure to
her body and brain. Jyoti Singh Pandey died from cardiac arrest,
from swelling in the brain and infections she could not overcome.'
Now is the time for Change to Protect our most basic human rights

ABOUT SUNNY JETSUN

Inspired by the sixties Sunny started traveling the world in 1970. His spiritual journey on the hippie trail to India took him through San Francisco, Los Angeles, London, Amsterdam, Paris, Vancouver, Sidney, and Kathmandu to Varanasi. His arrival on the sub-continent was the beginning of writing autobiographical verses capturing his travel experiences, encounters with remarkable people and his quest for self-realization. Combining experimentation with drugs, sex, rock & roll, meditation, Love and life in general. Sunny started to open up to a multi-dimensional Universe. He lived the mantra, "Turn on, tune in, drop out" realising Mind's-illusions, inspired by deeper feelings of holistic nature, empathy, energy & Space.

Over four decades Sunny has written and published 27 books of poetry, created over one hundred paintings, traveled the World and considers his masterpiece to be his daughter. He has spent the past fifteen years in Goa, India inspired by the freedom to experience and idealism of human consciousness.

Sunny Jetsun books and art are available on the web at:

Website: www.sunnyjetsun.com
Facebook: www.facebook.com/sunnyjetsun
Amazon: www.amazon.com/author/sunnyjetsun
Smashwords: www.smashwords.com/profile/view/sunnyjetsun

www.ingramcontent.com/pod-product-compliance
Lightning Source LLC
Chambersburg PA
CBHW020508030426
42337CB00011B/287